Preaching is Persuasion

HOW TO TEACH GOD'S WORD

Bryan J. Westra

INDIRECT KNOWLEDGE LIMITED
MURRAY, KENTUCKY

Indirect Knowledge Limited
2317 University Station
Murray, Kentucky 42071
www.indirectknowledge.com

Book Layout ©2014 Indirect Knowledge Limited

Ordering Information:
Quantity sales. Special discounts are available on quantity purchases by corporations, associations, and others. For details, contact the "Special Sales Department" at the address above.

Preaching is Persuasion/ Bryan J. Westra. —1st ed.
ISBN-13: 978-0-9899464-6-9

Contents

Dedicated to the most persuasive preachers I've had the privilege of working side-by-side with and learning from. Modeling your greatness has been an esteemed honor and blessed experience. As requested, your names will remain anonymous, and your teachings brought forth honestly.

"Every person lives by persuasions; things we believe."

—MIKE MURDOCK

DISCLAIMER

This book is designed to provide information and motivation to our readers. It is sold with the understanding that the publisher is not engaged to render any type of psychological, legal, or any other kind of professional advice. The content of each article is the sole expression and opinion of its author, and not necessarily that of the publisher. No warranties or guarantees are expressed or implied by the publisher's choice to include any of the content in this volume. Neither the publisher nor the individual author(s) shall be liable for any physical, psychological, emotional, financial, or commercial damages, including, but not limited to, special, incidental, consequential or other damages. Our views and rights are the same: You are responsible for your own choices, actions, and results. This book is designed to provide information on preaching and persuasion only. This information is provided and sold with the knowledge that the publisher and author do not offer any legal or other professional advice. In the case of a need for any such expertise consult with the appropriate professional. This book does not contain all information available on the subject. This book has not been created to be specific to any individual's or organizations' situation or needs. Every effort has been made to make this book as accurate as possible. However, there may be typographical and or content errors. Therefore, this book should serve only as a general guide and not as the ultimate source of subject information. This book contains information that might be dated and is intended only to educate and entertain. The author and publisher shall have no liability or responsibility to any person or entity regarding any loss or damage incurred, or alleged to have incurred, directly or indirectly, by the information contained in this book. You hereby agree to be bound by this disclaimer or you may return this book within the guarantee time period for a full refund.

INTRODUCTION

I've cracked the persuasion code for you. Now all you have to do is read this book and do what it says to do –and you'll preach as distinctly and persuasively as the most convincing preachers out there!

You see, making yourself more persuasive is as simple as modeling persuasive people; however, that being said, there's so much more to persuasion than most people will ever learn—even decent preachers. Understanding new and current persuasion models will give you the background needed to make sense of persuasion. In this book you'll discover how to preach more profoundly and winningly. You'll learn the secrets behind persuasion and how to implement these techniques yourself to instantly be more persuasive.

Here are just some of what you'll be learning throughout this book:

I. **Chapter 1** of this book starts with a thorough examination of psychological persuasion theories and models. Investigating these models is important if you want to acquire an intuitive sense of what persuasion is; how you can apply it; and how to use it in diverse contexts appropriately. These models have already been analyzed, scrutinized, and tested over and over again to prove themselves effective.

II. **Chapter 2** of this book explores some Neuro-Linguistic Models that elaborate on the importance of language patterns. I provide you some hypnotic persuasion patterns acquired from modeling some of the most persuasive preachers in the world. Some you may recognize; some you will not. These patterns help make any conversation more persuasive when infused with them.

III.   **Chapter 3** of this book explores persuasive storytelling techniques that plain and simply work. You won't believe how well in fact they work, until you find yourself applying these newfound skills with astonishing success.

IV.   **Chapter 4** of this book teaches you how to architect a persuasive sermon in just 20 minutes. Best part is—this method will change you; instantly making you ten-times more persuasive than you could ever hope to be. You'll be able to persuade your flock to do anything you want, and have them loving you for it!

V.   **Chapter 5** of this book closes by coming full circle and teaching you the art of modeling other persuasive preachers. The three methods you'll learn will have you consciously and unconsciously modeling the experts in no time flat. In this chapter I won't just be feeding you; I'll be teaching you how to feed yourself.

Everywhere, throughout this book, you'll discover valuable gold-nuggets that will change the way you preach forever. You'll reach more people; that is certainly to say, bring more people to the Lord. You'll instantly become more charismatic while allowed to be yourself. You'll captivate, hypnotize, and entrance crowds of people with your preaching—leaving them totally spellbound!

When I write a book I sometimes write if from a place of consciousness while other times find myself writing it in a very unconscious manner. The best of both sides of me come forward! My logical disposition is to structure lessons for you in such a way you can consciously comprehend them. Another part of me sometimes takes over though which dissolve unspoken rules; that is they are forgotten and I let other mind do the writing and teaching in a very unconscious manner. This is a phenomenon that happens to the people you'll be preaching to, while they listen to your sermons—moreover it happens to you all the time without your realizing it, as well, and will do so during the times when you deliver your effectively impactful sermons.

The knowledge you learn from this book is unlike other books that teach you how to preach persuasively and construct sermons. This approach you're going to learn in this book is cutting edge and goes to the root of persuasion and takes you step-by-step by the hand; teaching you the best practices when it comes to applying this knowledge practically.

The journey in writing this book has been a long and tedious one. Modeling the most persuasive preachers in the world is something I wanted to get right, and knew I must get right. Anything this necessary takes time to develop most would agree. I felt this way and therefore took painstaking steps to ensure the release of this book would accomplish what you, the reader, expected. Absolutely no short-cuts have been taken, and nothing has been kept back.

If you haven't already done so, I suggest you reserve a special place on your bookshelf for this exclusive book; because this book no-less will be a much loved resource, a favorite resource for most preachers, and one which will help you build your church on 'good-ground'.

EVERYTHING YOU NEED TO KNOW TO PREACH PERSUASIVELY AND LOVINGLY IS IN THIS BOOK. YOU NEED ONLY FLIP THE PAGES TO DISCOVER THE SECRET LESSONS HIDDEN INSIDE. NOTHING IS HELD BACK. I PROMISE.

CHAPTER 1

The Language of Persuasion is God (Part 1)

Only what we keep hearing do we believe. The Bible says, "In the beginning was the Word and the Word was with God, and the Word was God" (John 1:1). Take that to mean what is says; namely, because, I will be teaching you in the pages to come, exactly how powerful words can be, and specifically how you can use words to influence the persuasions of others, in your ministry. I am, in truth, going to teach you about the psychology of persuasion; in so much, that you learn how to use language to create beliefs and attitudes, and shape intentions, inspire motivations, and make others behave the way you wish for them to act. I want to impress upon you, to consider the convictions you're beginning to feel right now, as you're starting to get into these lessons, because maybe, just maybe, that's a revelation coming forward, within you, making you realize how a message, like the Bible, the most published book in all of human history, has been what so many have consistently believed, to the extent they have heard its powerful messages. Let this set the tone, for our great, little, journey, throughout this chapter and the ones to come.

I am going to start, by teaching you about the two types of persuasion. The first being systematic and the second heuristic. Next, we'll cover various models of persuasion. Then we'll look at some ideas on how you might apply these theories in your preaching ministry. This is to set the stage for chapter two, where you'll be learning some critical language lessons that will help you actually speak more persuasively.

Systematic Persuasion Theory

Systematic persuasion is the theory that people, when tasked with high-involvement decision-making conditions, tend to care less about what the communicator looks like, or how likeable they happen to be, and tend to make decisions based more on critical cognitions regarding information presented to them. In other words, it is how sound the information arguments happens to be, that determines if the arguments persuade the message receiver to agree or disagree.

To persuade someone under such conditions requires more engagement and a longer period of presenting arguments from the message giver. Another, relative point to make mention of, is to note that the more expert, the message giver appears to be, when delivering the argument, though not of primary importance in the persuasion process, it does still play a secondary role in persuading the subject (i.e., message receiver) to agree with the arguments. Not so important however is the likeability or attractiveness of the persuader.

Why this is Important?

Understanding systematic persuasion is important, because, as a preacher, you will run into situations, sometimes, where you are presenting more fact based arguments to your audience, and when this is the case; this is to say, when the involvement and critical faculty of your audience is highly involved in assessing what you are saying, it will be required of you to put in extra effort and time to influence them to agree with your arguments. During these types of interactions you will be more an educator, and less a presenter.

Case Study

In the early 1980s, a researcher at the University of Toronto, by the name of Shelly Chaiken, conducted research into heuristic versus systematic persuasion. Afterward, she published her findings in the Journal of Personality and Social

Psychology. Her report was titled, *Heuristic Versus Systematic Information Processing and the Use of Source Versus Message Cues in Persuasion.*

I want to share, at this time, the findings she discovered pertaining to the systematic persuasion portions of her research. Essentially, what Chaiken looked at was an experiment where she had developed these persuasive messages, and introduced this experiment to students at the University of Toronto. Her sample, was just over 200 students, and the persuasive messages were delivered by two different persuasion artists. One of the persuaders was dumbed-down and intentionally made to appear as unlikeable and disheveled, while the other was dressed professionally, cleaned up, and who presented the persuasive arguments in a very likeable fashion, building rapport with the message receivers.

The messages were comprised of either six or two persuasive arguments that concerned one of two different topics. The findings of the research, as it pertained to systematic persuasion theory was that when it came to the number of arguments; namely, one being greater in terms of six, and the other being lesser in terms of involvement, as only two arguments were to be considered by the students, they determined that a higher response of the involvement in terms of the number of arguments, made it so that the students wanted later discussion about these particular message topics at some future point. When it came to low involvement subjects, where only two arguments were to be considered, the students preferred to talk on a completely different topic altogether, dismissing future conversations on the low involvement arguments. Essentially, what this means, is that the students who were exposed to a higher involvement, i.e. systematic persuasion scenarios, actually needed more time to process through the arguments themselves. This is what they actually wanted.

So it took more time to persuade the students. I'll tell you a personal story in a moment, involving a time when I was in sales, when I had moved from being a sales professional, selling advertising to businesses, giving short, low involvement presentations (i.e., all that was required to sell the ads), to actually giving more involved presentations, during workshops, for the purpose of selling back of the room products, after the workshop seminar was over. I'll get into that, and explain to you the hurdles I had to overcome, and why all of this is so important to understand. For not, just understand that with systematic information processing, and specifically what this research proved to be true, is that the more involved, and the greater the number of arguments, the more time is needed to believe the arguments as being true. This means, that you need to take more time, to allow the arguments to become accepted as valid and true for the message receiver.

Another interesting note, to make mention of, is during this experimentation, Chaiken discovered it doesn't necessarily matter, when it comes to systematic persuasion, what the actual expert giving the arguments particularly looked like, or even what the person's attitude toward the message receiver happened to be. The effectiveness did not change, even when the persuasion artist was not so nice, or calculated in their approach.

What also is worth mentioning, which Chaiken discusses, is research conducted by Cacioppo, a year earlier in 1979, which touches on how high involvement persuasion hurt the likelihood of the persuasion amongst participants. It is important to understand that these different persuasion theories have their own place. Depending on the specific context and the hierarchy of the authority figure, will depend on which models of persuasion are applied to be most effective in a given context.

One last point I want to bring to your attention is the persuasion principle of The Sleeper Effect. The sleeper effect is a phenomenon which occurs when an argument, such like television advertisements work to convey, in which a discounting clue is asserted (e.g., disclaimer, income disclosure, etc.) that may in the short term work against the advertised argument, but which over time actually is forgotten, to allow the argument to remain in the subject's (message-receiver) mind, affecting their opinion. This is what happens a lot of times in political campaigns, where the campaign ad may assert, "Paid for by X"; where X is the name of the party running against the candidate they are seeking to destroy in the advert. The subject (message-receiver) may at first dismiss the advert as being a smear campaign, instantly dismissing the credibility of the advertisement, but as time goes on, over the course of the campaign, this aspect (i.e., "Paid for by X") is forgotten, and the message has sense influenced and changed the opinion of the subject (message-receiver).

In Chaiken's research, she suggests that both extremely low and high levels of involvement do not set the stage for inducing the sleeper effect. She also ends on the note of relaying how though high involvement may not gain immediate compliance from the subject, persuading them to take a different position, it does have longer term stick value than low involvement persuasion in which the personality of the message giver is taken into more account in the persuasion process.

What You Need to Know?

It has been a number of years ago, but I had been in the world of professional selling, giving expert sales presentations to clients, and doing quite well. The involvement wasn't really all that high, in terms of what was required for the potential customer to make a decision to buy my product or not. I ran into a problem eventually. The problem I faced was I eventually found myself presenting at workshops. These workshops were delivered, with the intention of selling products on the back end of these workshops. My selling ability, i.e. ability to persuade my audience to buy the products at the end of the presentation dropped overnight compared to when I gave those earlier sales presentations. I had given those thousands of times, and now, I could not for the life of me, figure out why I wasn't having much success with these seminar style workshop presentations; selling these less costly, back of the room products. I thought I had lost my mojo, but what I had failed to realize was the higher involvement happening amongst workshop participants, from what was the case when I sold those other less involved decision making criteria products to business leaders.

I thought my clean looks, likeability, and charismatic personality was enough, but it most certainly wasn't. It was definitely a shock to my ego. I was really failing at capably being able to make the sales targets the company had superimposed on me.

Well, one day, I awoke late in the morning, just ten minutes before I was to present. I had a hotel room in the same hotel, you see, which I was to present the workshop materials from. I didn't have time to shower, barely enough time to put my wrinkled shirt and pants on, and then get down to the presentation hall. I remember feeling really unprofessional, and quite self-conscious when I walked in that huge room.

When I stepped into the room, I must have been the worst dressed in the place. In that moment, something snapped inside me, and I decided I didn't care how I looked. I was disgusted with myself for not doing my job well, and had made up my mind this would be my last workshop, because I was quitting. I turned my attention on really working with each group interactively, helping to clarify and explain each point, acting as an expert, and caring less about making the sale. My job became to present the logical advantages of using the tools we sold afterward, and why it was a good idea to buy them, and all the minute details. I had all that down. I just had thought it was less important spending so much time going over details, and more important to sell the emotional benefits. I was wrong.

At the end of the workshop, nearly everyone purchased, and I remember we actually ran out of products and had to take orders on a cheap notepad, capturing addresses and other customer details in order to send them out in the mail.

When I reached my hotel room, soon after the workshop, before I could even step into the shower, my phone rang. It was my boss, and he congratulated me. He told me when he saw me enter the room disheveled, he had made up his mind at that moment to fire me after the workshop. He said he changed his mind, of course, when everything sold out, because he knew he couldn't afford to lose me.

My point for telling you this story is to impress upon you the difference in presentation situations where you may find yourself preaching. In the first situation I merely gave presentations in which my job was mostly to build rapport and present myself as a likeable fellow. I had been taught that actually saying less, was best; namely, because it was possible to talk yourself out of a sale. In the second situation, I was presenting a product that required a high amount of customer involvement. The product was complex, and it had to be very well explained how this product could be used to help the potential customer. The extra time I put in working with workshop participants, and involving them more with my compelling arguments, the more this approach to persuasion worked in my favor.

What you essentially need to know about systematic persuasion is that it is a persuasion theory that requires less of you in terms of personality and how you present yourself in terms of likeability. The persuasion is influenced based on how the subject conceptualizes, because there is a greater level of involvement in making sense of what you're persuading them to take action on doing. For example, you may be preaching sermon on tithing, and find that you need to be much more an expert on presenting the ideas of tithing from an authoritative biblical perspective, and less from the position of nicely asking your congregation to pay their ten percent. It really all depends, but you get the idea.

How to Systematically Persuade Your Audience?

When I think of systems, I think of unique processes for breaking down large chunks of information, down into bite-size chunks, which can be more clearly understood and applied. In applying systematic persuasion techniques, the idea is essentially the same. Here is how we achieve implementing systematic persuasion techniques:

First, you want to consider when you might need to apply systematic processing. Here is a list of things to keep in mind, which are likely scenarios of when you would need to apply systematic persuasion:

- Whenever your subject (i.e., message-receiver) will need to put in careful consideration. People consider ideas in order to generate judgment confidence.
- Times when you might need to have your subject consider something random and unexpected. These types of scenarios usually require more thoughtful consideration in order for your subject to sell themselves on your ideas.
- During particular topics that personally or directly affect the subject, or topics which are close to them psychologically. The more relevant your persuasion ideas are to the subject (i.e., message-receiver) the more time and concentration they will likely require to determine if they are on board or not.
- Anytime a subject (i.e., message-receiver) disagrees immediately outright with your proposition or ideas, and it causes their critical faculty to raise a red-flag and reject your ideas. Taking a systematic persuasion approach is one great way to drip your message on them until which time, they have had time to process it from multiple angles, and accept what you say as being the most reasonable solution or option.

Step two, requires you to take a look at your persuasive message. In doing so, you want to look at it from a rational perspective, and consider how your subjects might intellectualize it as being. Intellectualization is applied by your subject, often, as it is a defense mechanism many people will naturally apply to block out their emotional unconscious feelings, so that they may make a rational decision. This is especially true, when the subject is faced with making a high involvement decision. If you can ensure that your logic is sound and in no way circular logic or faulty logic, then it will go a long way in your favor in terms of persuading your subject (i.e., message-receiver).

The last step is to use someone uninvolved, as a sounding board, to be objective and honest in relaying how they perceive your offer or persuasion message to be. You can then take their feedback and go-back and modify your persuasive argument, refining it as needed, before you deliver it to your intended target audience.

What if You Were to Apply Systematic Theory?

The key thing to remember about any theory is it's theoretical, and this means it's speculative at best. You never completely know for sure how your intended audience will perceive your message or how persuaded they will be to take an action you request of them. This being said, one of the best ways to impact your ability to persuade your audience is through presenting a logical argument in a clearly conveyed message.

You stack the deck in your favor the more logically acceptable your persuasion argument is. The more you stack the deck in your favor, the more likely you'll receive your desired end result. As you may have juggled in your mind, this first theory, I'm presenting you with, starts with the basis of logical reasoning. I've given you this argument first, to impress upon you, to always consider in your mind, how you can find a logical basis for what you're presenting to people, even assuming you'll be presenting many arguments that are not founded in logic.

I think you'll find if you apply this system, even indirectly in your mind, to most of your persuasion arguments, even when it is not necessary to persuade your target audience into conforming to your ideology you'll stand a fair better

PREACHING IS PERSUASION • 9

chance of succeeding in swaying the audience, in unpredictable times. I've found that it's better to play it safe, than sorry.

Let's look now at the inverse, you might say, of Systematic Persuasion Theory, and learn about Heuristic Persuasion Theory. This next section takes a look at feelings, and the short-cuts subjects (i.e., message-receivers) take to make decisions and be persuaded by others' points of views and notions.

Heuristic Persuasion Theory

Heuristic persuasion deals with heuristics, which are the informal rules individuals use to make everyday decisions regarding, well, usually insignificant decisions, mainly about how they spend their time and what they choose to do with it. This could also include decisions regarding where they focus their energy. These heuristics act as innate guidelines for helping people quickly to make decisions, or reasonable guesses about what they should do or shouldn't do. Heuristics are habitual. Heuristics, are actually short-cuts we utilize when making seemingly easy decisions over having to rely on more complex decision making models. Heuristics solve a problem; that is to say, they keep us moving through life without us having to give much thought to the multitude of persuasive messages we encounter and are bombarded by every day of our lives.

Why is this Important?

Heuristics are important to learn about because heuristic persuasion focuses on inducing attitude change. Heuristics alter individual's evaluations of a target message through the use of these heuristic short-cuts.

Most often people do not take a lot of time to evaluate or exert a lot of attention or psychological resources when it comes to judging the validity of a particular persuasive message being relayed. The codicil to this, however, is that unless a persuasive message has a particular importance to us personally, most often we will rely on superficial cues and heuristics to simply assume the validity of what that persuasive message has to offer us.

From the context of selling, more and more often, now, sales professionals are adopting a soft-selling approach, as mechanism to influence and persuade potential customers to buy their products or services. In the world of advertising this is also an adopted approach, chosen my advertisers. When individuals are bombarded with various images that have certain representational meanings that evoke certain emotional responses, or which act as symbols that can be associated particular meanings, or for that matter values that promote the experience of owning a particular product or experiencing a particular service.

Heuristic persuasion can be very helpful, because the strategy is more assumptive and useful to the persuasion artist for this reason. Assumptions or presuppositions put limitations on the extent subjects are willing to go to make a decision or not. For this reason, when people make heuristic decisions they most often rely on their feelings, values, beliefs, instincts, and intuitions to judge the validity of a persuasive argument, and, in so doing, decide whether or not to act or not. Action, of course, can mean anything; for example, believing something is true, could be a desired action, which the persuasion artist would want as the outcome of his or her end result.

For your particular context, which is assumedly, the professional world of ministry; namely, ministering to a congregation or a small group of individuals who you'll be connecting with regularly, heuristics can be applied strategically to get your message across and accepted by the message receiver, i.e. your subject. As of now, I've used the word 'subject' to represent the congregant, or members of your ministry, who will be receiving your persuasive messages. Subjects is a generic term I'll continue using throughout the rest of this book, but for now you can simply assume your subject is a message receiver for your persuasive messages.

In the ministry, when it's important to get across God's laws, commandments, to teach people about right and wrong, and about the teachings of Jesus, and, perhaps, even their particular calling in the world of a Christ centered evangelistic ministry placement, you can use heuristics to convey matter-of-factly certain judgment calls which will bypass their critical faculty, i.e. their innate doubt and uncertainty mechanism, to have them receive and accept the truth as you present it from God, and His calling you to do so. This is powerful stuff—Heuristics!

Why else you need to understand heuristic persuasion, from a minister's perspective, is heuristics will help you build teams and be a more effective communicator as you develop and grow your own ministry. As a person of influence you already have a certain level of influence, already. Reading this book, and applying these lessons, will help you to show yourself approved, in the even you are ever challenged. Mostly, being the leader over others, will authorize you to make claims, often, without being challenged by the sheep who follow you. This is an applied leadership position you are in that puts you in control of how others think, believe, should act, and what their roles specifically are in your ministry. You are the chief operations officer, i.e. head-haunch-o, and you call the shots, so these lessons will help you in powerfully commanding authority over others much more easily. You'll definitely have an edge over others who might try and challenge your authority. The authority God has given you cannot be denied, and these persuasion lessons will ensure it never is.

Case Study

I want now to revisit the Chaiken case study. Her study delved into both systematic and heuristic examination. It is time, now, to focus on her findings, relating to heuristics.

Chaiken found that the message-deliverer was a key factor in how well respondents took to persuasive arguments and complied with heuristic persuasion messages. Her experiments found that the message-deliver impacted the persuasion. This means, for our purposes, that it is important, when delivering heuristic messages, that persuasion artists look authoritative, i.e. dress the part, that they act convincing, and are aligned with their message wholeheartedly. The message-receiver should sense the sincerity and innate-belief of the persuasion artist. For this reason, it is important to 'act-as-if'. Meaning, act as if you are sold, yourself, on your message. If you are not, your unconscious cues and non-verbal behavior will speak louder and more impactful than your words.

Keep in mind, her research showed that messages accepted through heuristic processing have a tendency to lose their efficacy over time. This is one reason why many congregants will get wrapped up in the message, the music, the experience of attending church, and donate large sums of money, and later experience cognitive dissonance, i.e. giver's remorse, questioning their actions to give money they may not have been able to afford to give away to your ministry. It is important to be the messenger and not the message giver. In other words, give all credit and glory to God Jesus, and avoid taking credit for these persuasive heuristic messages. Remember, it is the authority, the message deliver (i.e., God Jesus), that has a deeper meaning and therefore stronger hold over a congregants need to follow instructions. Presenting your arguments in this fashion ensures greater persuasive affect over those in your congregation.

What You Need to Know?

I remember, as a small child, visiting a church once, sitting in a Sunday school room, and being told the story of Saul who became Paul after his conversion. This story is one that I have never been able to forget, and I must have been about nine or ten years old when I first heard the story. It is very intriguing on many levels.

We begin the story looking at this man named Saul, who was a very prominent man in Jewish society. He was very much against early Christians, who were creating a presence. It says in Acts 8:1, "And Saul was consenting unto his death. And at that time there was a great persecution against the church which was at Jerusalem; and they were all scattered abroad throughout the regions of Judaea and Samaria, except the apostles." By "his death" is meant Stephen. This is evident back in Acts 7:59 "And they stoned Stephen, calling upon God, and saying, Lord Jesus, receive my spirit." See Stephen was a devout Christian. He was a true follower of Jesus, and even during his death; death by stoning, he still remained faithful to Jesus being God. In fact, we find in this section, just before his death, he actually asks the Lord to not hold those committing the sin responsible. But, Saul, a devout Jew, strong in his Jewish faith, consented to the death of Stephen. He was okay with it. Saul, perceived the teaching of early Christianity as heresy, and a threat to the Jews. He even went so far to get permission to force men and women out of their homes to be brought to prison, for their Christian beliefs.

In Acts 7: 55 we learn that Stephen looks up toward heaven, and sees Jesus standing next the right hand of God. He goes on, in verse 56, to declare, "Look! I see the heavens opened and the Son of Man standing at the right hand of God!" Stephen is, in awe, making a declaration of what he sees, and at this point, the Jews stopped listening to him, and proceed to rush at him. After this Stephen is stoned to death, a horrendous death, indeed.

If we go visit some of the verses, specifically dealing with Saul, we learn in Acts 7: 58 that the witnesses of Stephen's death, laid down their clothes, at the feet of a young man named Saul. Saul, was there.

We're beginning here with a character, in a situation and a scene, in which we have an early Christian individual. This individual, named Stephen, who is being stoned to death. As he's being stoned to death he is so firm and resolute in his beliefs that he is actually praying for his persecutors, those Jews condemning him to death by stoning, not be held responsible for their sins.

Saul, we observe, consents to this murder. He is okay with it. He believes murdering this individual is the right thing to do. So we see an early glimpse of Saul's life, and how he is living his life in a normal, everyday, routine. He was Jewish. He was firmly Jewish. He was resolute in his Jewish beliefs. He was completely against Christianity. He abhorred Christians. In fact, he had gone so far as to gain permission from the high priest, obtaining letters of permission, that he could go to peoples' homes, who were Christian, and yank them out of their homes, and bound them and bring them to Jerusalem.

He was on his way, near to Damascus, searching out anyone who may be adhering to these heretical Christian beliefs, and something happened. Something that is mystifying. Something that many people today would find utterly unimaginable, yet, completely miraculous. It starts with a question.

> This question is, according to Acts 9:4, "And he fell to the earth, and heard a voice saying unto him, Saul, Saul, why persecutest thou me?"

This voice was the voice of none other than Jesus.

This was just after the everyday normal routine this man, Saul, stepping forward, to do what he did so well, which was persecute Christians. It was normal routine for him.

Saul was firmly resolute in his beliefs. It say's in Acts 8:3, "As for Saul, he made havock of the church, entering into every house, and haling men and women committed them to prison." "And Saul, yet breathing," this is found in Acts 9:1, "And Saul, yet breathing out threatenings and slaughter against the disciples of the Lord, went unto the high priest," confirming what I've said, so far.

In Acts 9:4, to say again, what Jesus says, "And he fell to the earth, and heard a voice saying unto him, Saul, Saul, why persecutest thou me?" We see in Acts 9:8, that then, "And Saul arose from the earth; and when his eyes were opened, he saw no man: but they led him by the hand, and brought him into Damascus."

This was his conversion. This was truly a conversion that Saul underwent. We go on to learn that Saul becomes Paul, and that he goes from trying to destroy the church, putting men and women into prison, for their faith; to being a completely different individual altogether. All because of one, single, solitary, incident that happened on the way to Damascus. Get that, it's huge!

Traveling along the road to Damascus a light from heaven flashing down on him, forcing him to fall to the ground, and then a simple question: "Saul, Saul, why persecutest thou me?"

Saul asks, "Who art thou, Lord?" Questioning the Lord Jesus back in Acts 9:5. "Who art thou, Lord?"

And God replies still in Acts 9:5, "I am Jesus whom thou persecutest: it is hard for thee to kick against the pricks."

Then in Acts 9:6, "And he trembling and astonished said, Lord, what wilt thou have me to do? And the Lord said unto him, Arise, and go into the city, and it shall be told thee what thou must do."

Of course, the men traveling with him, they were speechless. The Bible in Acts 9:7 says, "And the men which journeyed with him stood speechless, hearing a voice, but seeing no man."

When Saul got up from off the ground, he was blind, unable to even see the men, who led him by the hand, taking him to Damascus. Then for three days, Saul, remained without his site. And I'll stop here.

What I want to expound on is the idea a simple soft-sell; it was just a miraculous happening, to be spoken to by Jesus. He spoke with a voice that could be heard and understood. Blinded by a bright light, simply asking a question, of God, and it was enough to turn this man who had impeccable faith in his own Jewish beliefs, in the teachings that he had been taught his entire life. Everything he knew and understood, as real, as evidenced by his beliefs, and, yet, one thing, came along, and changed all of that. One thing changed this entire man's life. And he became a leader in the early Christian church, being a missionary who went all throughout the lands; creating churches, recruiting people into those churches, both Jews and Gentiles. In fact, Paul is credited with allowing Jews and Gentiles to eat together, which at the time was completely unorthodox. Jews couldn't eat with Gentiles. It was the unthinkable.

So why do I tell this story? Why is this important, now? The answer is it only takes a question. It only takes a question to change a person's life. It is too much to think about. I mean, think about it. Really contemplate this in your mind for a moment, because it goes to the heart of heuristic persuasion.

Imagine yourself in Saul's shoes. You had just consented to a man's death by stoning. Forcing this man out of a city by brute force, and then brutally stoning him to death. Agreeing with the mob that it was okay. Feeling okay about that action. Feeling justified and right. Feeling as though your intentions were completely justified.

Everyday routine.

Just going about my business. Same ole same ole.

Until something happens!

Till the voice of God called him to be something different. Brought him on a different journey. Changed the direction of his life. Forever!

Saul, himself, even was imprisoned being a Christian advocate; multiple times, in fact. Just advocating himself as a Christian, and sharing that Jesus Christ is Lord and Savior; in fact, the Christ!

Everyday routine.

Just going about my business.

And then the voice of God calls unto me, asking, a simple question: Why?

I had no choice but to listen, as I was blinded by the bright light. I'm down here on the ground. The dusty road to Damascus. Feeling the heat of the light shining down on me. And there a customer comes.

"...Saul, Saul, why persecutest thou me?"

"...why persecutest thou me?"

I mean, put yourself in those shoes for just a moment.

Now when we get into the next chapter of this book, we'll talk about language in a lot more detail. What I want to share now, however, is that the question

Why(?) is a question you have to be careful using. Because, why, instantly puts someone on the defensive, causing them to defend their position. Of course, if someone is defending their position, it means they are against another position. The word why is concrete, cementing whatever is asked.

Here we have a question asked by Jesus, to Saul: "Saul, Saul, why persecutest thou me?"

I mean, how would you reply to something like that? If you say, for example, "I persecute you because..." and give a logical reason, to defend your position, even answering presupposes you must believe that Jesus is the Christ. Think of the brilliant intelligence behind that one question. Even, answering that question, even acknowledging that that question was asked, presupposes you must believe in Jesus as the Christ.

The only that Saul could do is ask a question back. But, what question, would one ask? What question would be the most logical, being put on the spot by Jesus in Heaven, to ask?

The question Saul asked was: "Who art thou, Lord?"

Jesus did not ask a question back, rather he answered directly. He answered: "I am Jesus whom thou persecutest: it is hard for thee to kick against the pricks."

Now I don't know about you, but, a situation like that, makes it fairly easy for me to believe Jesus Christ is Lord.

Just a simple question.

And a question back.

And then an answer.

"Who art thou, Lord?" asked Saul.

Jesus simply says, "I am Jesus whom thou persecutest."

What a revelation. What an upheaval in a person's life. Just a soft-sell. There wasn't any instruction beyond that conversation, except: "...Arise, and go into the city, and it shall be told thee what thou must do."

I mean, just think of the enormity of just that. It's gigantic.

Just going about my everyday routine and bam, something happens. Something that sets my entire life off course, happens. Going to Damascus, becoming baptized in the name of Jesus, getting my sight back after three days of being in the dark, and becoming, in the process, a true devout Christian. A true devout follower of Christ.

Then going on to become a major leader in the Church, persecuted by others, but resolute firmly in one's belief —and, it started with a simple question!

Just a soft-sell.

The reason now, and I'll stop going and on for a moment, that I tell this story, is because it is one I can still remember from early childhood. It had a profound impact on my existence. It stands out in my mind, and I see the happening, happening, as if I were living it. I like the story very much.

The reason I tell it is, because, like with heuristics, it can be a simple question someone asks, and those preconceived short-cut ideas we have in our heads can either dismiss the story as being fraudulent and untrue, or tell us that it is the way it happened, without us having to give much structural thought about it.

Being led by the hand, by men in your entourage, to Damascus, and left with nothing else to focus on, except, the experience of what just happened. Walking along the road to Damascus, holding hands with men, unsure about my future, and then having to think about and contemplate what just happened. That is a soft-sell. A sell that starts with a question, ends with an answer. Nothing overly profound, although the experience itself is profound —miraculous one might argue. And then...You're in a whole new world. You're faced with obstacles you can't see. One mission in mind: To serve God! To serve as a missionary. A church builder. A writer. And certainly, the writings of Paul are very persuasive, teaching and instructing what churches should do and not do. Building up a reputation as a Christian. Oh Saul from Tarsus, you did a lot of traveling, and a lot for the body of Christ. But, walking that road to Damascus!

God didn't have to say a lot for you to do a lot.

God didn't have to say a lot to persuade Saul to completely do a 180 degree turn; turning away from everything he had believed up to that critical day in his life. Now listen to me. God only had to ask one question, only. That's it.

Now one question may not sound like anything spectacular, but I want you to reconsider that for a moment. I want you to suspend your disbelief and put aside what you think you know about persuasion. Take a leap of faith with me. After all, if you just have to doubt something, doubt something that serves you no possible good. Really get this, because it's a lot more profound than the masked simplicity that secretly guards its truth. It's nothing at all what it looks like. A question, changed a man's life. Do you believe?

There wasn't a lot of contemplation. There wasn't any systematic thinking involved. Not at all. There wasn't thinking about, well what about this, or what if this is just a ploy to get me to believe about this. None of that.

Just a simple question.

A simple question: Why?

Brilliantly rendered by Jesus.

Remember, reader, it is just as easy to ask why not, as it is to ask why, but you'll always get a different answer.

You have choices, and that's what everyone has, but the problem is most people only see what's in front of them, what they've known from the past, and make decisions based on their model of the world. The good news for you is that it only takes one person, asking the right question, to change another person's life. And when you ask that question, you become the change others are looking forward to embracing. And this creates value in you, and what you have to say.

When it comes to heuristics, it really is simple. What is the theory behind heuristics? The answer is you're dealing with people's emotions, not their rational, logical thinking brain. You're touching something inside them that they perceive truth in, but can't rationalize. It feels right. It feels like the right path to be on. It becomes an easy decision, because you don't actually have to stop and think about the pros and cons and weigh everything out. People have these shortcuts established already within them. We all do.

For example, if someone goes to sell you something, and you've never heard of that brand, you instantly think what? It's less valuable, I've never heard of it. Or, better yet, when someone goes to sell you something, and then after pitching it to you, tells you, "Well, you can get it for less. I'll drop the price." What do you instantly feel inside you about the product? Here's a hint...You feel less value! These are the shortcuts, also called heuristics, I'm talking about. Jesus didn't reason with Saul.

Jesus did not reason with Saul!

Jesus appealed to his emotions and Saul bought what Jesus was offering, before knowing what he was buying. Incredibly fascinating and astonishing I find this to be. I love this story. Love it!

I wonder if you, reading this book, would like to be as persuasive as Jesus, in your own preaching and interpersonal communications? If so, let's turn our attention now onto how to use heuristics.

How to Heuristically Persuade Your Audience?

The first thing you must do to use heuristics effectively, is understand weaknesses heuristics possess. Heuristics are mental shortcuts, which allow your subjects to make quick decisions, without thinking cognitively. One way I like to look at heuristics it to think of them like the rules of thumb we utilize to solve many of life's problems. It is the way we assume is right, based on past experiences, and framed around who is actually delivering to us a persuasive message; in other words, more important is the messenger, than the message itself.

The weakness, as you might guess, is that hasty decisions do not always produce desired results. A fast talking, very persuasive, all smiles, salesman, is perhaps leading you down a path you may agree to today, but regret tomorrow. This is the essence of Social Psychologist, Leon Festinger's work on cognitive dissonance; namely, what we call buyer's remorse. It is internal conflict, a discord we feel within ourselves, that causes us to feel the emotion regret.

So the first thing, and this really goes to the heart of all persuasion, is intent. What is your intention for affecting someone emotionally? Is it to help them? Is it to cause them pain? Is it to destroy them? Persuasion is preaching to the heart as well as the mind of someone, to the extent that they are altered, and the change leads them to take some type of action, which in return brings about some type of consequence. An end result, let me tell you, is first step to developing any persuasive message. Understanding this is the 100 level college course on persuasion. Where we are at, even so early in this book, is remarkably, PH.D level material.

Here are all the steps to instantly put heuristics to work in your persuasion messages:

I.   Step 1, consider the mental habits of your audience.

II.   Step 2, consider what their beliefs are.

III.   Step 3, determine the process by which attitudes or beliefs will be changed as you appeal to these habits or emotions.

IV.   Step 4, asset in your message, how your audience members, or subjects, should not be so critical. We hear people often say, "You're being awfully critical!" When someone tells someone else this, they are actually being persuasively judgmental, indirectly implying that being critical is a negative behavior to exhibit. Please understand this point, dear reader, as it's important to understand.

V.   Step 5, embed heuristics and trite statements into your persuasion arguments, i.e. your sermons, and by doing so, you'll be stacking the deck in your favor, persuasively speaking.

An example, to carry this forth better, might be that you determine that your audience aren't quick to be coming off their money. You determine that they are quick to judge anything anyone says about paying forth an offering of money. The process to change this belief requires, pointing out to your subject that being critical of the idea of selfishly holding onto money, keeps you from being able to ascertain more of the things in life you value most. Things like a good relationship with Jesus. You may remind them about the story of the wealthy man, who's God was money. They will make certain indirect inferences associating this story with their unwillingness to give up something that they may receive something else. You may then look at the audience peripherally, and tell them, talking to them all as if you were talking to just one person, how they look like the most critical people you've ever seen (jokingly of course). Then you may tell them you knew someone who felt exactly like they do, but found that when he/she gave money, they found that God had mysteriously and supernaturally blessed them beyond anything they could imagine. Notice, in this last sentence how we're embedding heuristics like, beyond imagination, which is essentially implying don't think critically, because this is beyond critical thinking. You'll of course, talk about how some things are beyond our understanding, and how sometimes we just have to have faith. Make faith a valuable virtue, and lack of faith something that holds people back from having success. The associations are that blind faith = a good thing, while lack of faith = a bad thing. Those that believe in Jesus blindly, are better off than the person who criticizes others for not realistically looking at the falsity of science and reason brings with it, which robs people of their faith, and causes them to live a miserable, depressed existence, with no hope of salvation—a hell.

What if You Were to Apply Heuristic Theory?

Certainly, I can only speak from my own experiences; however, I know you know yourself, well enough, to know what can happen if you apply something important into your preaching. Many of the most sought-after preachers, those who earn the most rewards from their preaching, apply this very theory into their preaching ministries.

Think about what you've just learned, and really consider, truly consider it all, and conceptualize how you might instantly apply heuristic persuasion techniques. I'm not suggesting you apply it as I've suggested you do, as maybe you have something else in mind. Something in your mind that will help you get one step further, successfully, in your ministry, can come about, and surface, even when you're not fully thinking about it. Imagine, if you take a few minutes now, to wonder how you can come up with some immediate ideas and adopt a heuristic approach to improving the quality of your preaching. Would you be able to bring more people into the fold, or perhaps would you be able to persuade your sheep to give more to the ministry, so that you could bring more people to Christ Jesus?

Everybody learns differently, and one thing is for sure, by now, is that you're gaining internal resources, which will give you more possibility and understanding when it comes to influencing others. Your scope is expanding, that is to say. Keep thinking, even if you have to do so unconsciously, because now it is time to focus on next section of this chapter.

Models of Persuasion

Over time, various models of persuasion have been developed, to help us understand persuasion; specifically, why people do what they do as it pertains to three inextricably associated concepts. These concepts are: (a) beliefs, (b) behaviors, and (c) attitudes. These conceptions work together to persuade people to believe certain ideas, these beliefs create certain feelings and attitudes, which create a reaction or action that we call behavior.

In the following models we'll investigate are hypothetical. They are based on research and experimentation, as well as non-experimental and quasi-experimental research. Learning these models will give you the ability to experiment on your own, to find what models work and don't work for your particular circumstances. In essence you can decide for yourself what is valid, keeping that only; while dismissing what is not valid.

As we navigate the following models, most important is you keep in mind the essence of these models: (a) beliefs, (b) behaviors, and (c) attitudes. These should be kept in the back of your mind. One strategy I have adopted for keeping these in mind, which you may find useful, has been to understand that that words create thoughts, thoughts repeated create beliefs, beliefs create attitudes, and attitudes create reactions, which lead to behavior (i.e., actions). This chain, is, in my mind, a formula for affecting change in people.

Why Learn Persuasion Models?

As a preacher, you'll be talking to many personality types. People come from different backgrounds. They have different primary beliefs, and secondary beliefs. They have different attitudes about how information should be presented. Your listeners also have differing intentions about why they are listening to your message. People have different motivations for listening to you. Lastly, they behave differently, as a result of the messages they receive from you. Keep in mind, persuasion is the attempt to influence a person's beliefs, attitudes, intentions, motivations, or behaviors.

You want to learn these persuasion models so that you can be versatile in presenting your messages effectively. By effectively, I mean you want to achieve your ability to persuade, i.e. change your subjects' beliefs, attitudes, intentions, motivations, or behaviors.

Every sermon you preach has a different desired outcome. Now, normally, these outcomes have a single indirect thread of purpose that runs through them all. For example, if you're a pulpit pastor, leading a church, your common thread is leading your flock to live Godly lives. If you're preaching to missionaries in a remote part of the world, your common thread would be to develop missionaries to bring forth salvation to all parts of the world.

Generally speaking, however, each message is created with a single purposeful outcome in mind. It may be to encourage your congregation to tithe regularly. It may be to teach Godly values. It may be to teach about right and wrong behavior, and how God feels about that. My point is there's a central purpose for each message; yet, an overall intention behind why you are preaching to that particular group of individuals.

These models of persuasion help you elicit changes in beliefs, attitudes, intentions, motivations, or behaviors; serving, what you might refer to as: God's purpose for them.

What You Need to Know?

In this section we'll be covering the following models: (a) Attribution Model, (b) Conditioning Model, (c) Cognitive Dissonance Model, (d) Elaboration Likelihood Model, (e) Functional Model, (f) Inoculation Model, (g) Narrative Transportation Model, and (h) the Social Judgment Model. Understand, these are theoretical models; meaning, they are abstract representations of various research. You should remember, when applying or testing any theory, that what's important is the outcome. So keep the end in mind, always, as that's what's purposeful for achieving persuasion excellence.

The Attribution Model

The first model of persuasion I want to teach you about is The Attribution Model. The Attribution Model is founded on the work of social psychologist Fritz Heider. He is also titled with being the Father of Attribution Theory. He has an interesting background, worth checking out sometime, but for the sake of brevity I want to teach you about Attribution theory from an applied perspective.

When I was in college, working on my MBA in Marketing, I went in depth learning about how companies formulate brand promises and formulate their slogans based around the promise that their brand offers consumers.

The fascinating thing is in one of the models I studied, I learned that a brand promise starts with certain attributes that a product possesses; that make it uniquely separate from other products. For example, an attribute in the world of professional selling, these are also often referred to as features or functions that a product possesses. In branding, in particular, however, we start with attributes, and these attributes are the qualities of a particular brand. They are essentially what make a product completely unique in the marketplace.

Let's look at an example to learn how a brand promise is devised. A micro-wave-oven may have several distinct attributes. My personal microwave has a feature that allows me to take down the temperature intensity (wattage output). If I want to cook enchiladas, which have been frozen and packaged into a micro-wavable meal, I have to take the intensity down by half the usual wattage. I do this so the meal cooks at the ideal setting, so I don't burn the food. So this is one attribute my microwave possesses.

Another attribute my microwave has is a black color with stainless steel ac-centuations. Yet another attribute my microwave has is a turntable, which rotates to cook the food more optimally.

These are three of the primary attributes my microwave possesses that I recall immediately off the top of my head. These attributes, in order to get to the brand promise; that is, what the promise of this particular microwave's product brand happens to be, requires me to start with these unique attributes I've mentioned. The next step is to ladder up. So from attributes, I'm then going to go up to ad-vantages of these particular attributes, and this takes me to the next level, which are the logical advantages of these particular attributes.

For me personally, the attribute color (i.e., black with stainless steel trim), the logical advantage to me is that they fit into my kitchen scheme. I have a stainless steel sink, and other items in my kitchen that make this color scheme a good choice. When I made the decision to buy this particular microwave I either con-sciously or unconsciously took this into account as a factor when making a buy-ing decision. Another attribute; namely, wattage change, and though this probably wasn't a conscious decision, but rather an unconscious decision, as I don't honestly recall this as a factor for buying the microwave, as it hasn't been that long ago, but it is a feature that works very well with the ethnic foods that I eat. Many of the microwave dinners, in fact many that I eat on a weekly basis, the temperature is suggested to be taken down to half what it usually is. This allows me to cook the food to the best quality that a microwave can produce for these particular meals. The last attribute, the turntable feature, is very important to me. The times in my life, when I owned microwave ovens, which did not possess this attribute, I had problems cooking many types of microwavable meals. Those other microwaves had a tendency to burn the foodstuffs I cooked. One example you may be able to relate with is microwave popcorn. One side cooks well, while the side on the bottom burns. The burn-smell then emanates throughout the rest of the bag, spoiling the popcorn eating experience. These are all logical advantages that solve logical problems.

Revisiting for a moment, our lesson on structural processing theory, which has people making logical, thought-out decisions, based on cognitive processing of the pros and cons of a persuasion message; here we have people making logical decisions based around their needs and desire to solve a problem by purchasing a solution or answer to that problem in the form of a product or service. They weigh the pros and cons to determine what type of impact this particular advantage will serve in shoring up that potential problem.

Next we go up our metaphoric ladder, yet, another rung, which brings us to the emotional benefit a particular logical advantage has. These benefits we determine by asking, how is this going to affect the consumer emotionally? We go back to the design elements, being the black and stainless steel fitting into my kitchen theme. This makes me feel balanced and peaceful, as well as more comfortable in my home. They also make me feel as though I have good taste. These are things reflective of how I personally feel about myself. I'm congruently aligned with these attributes emotionally. It is also nice when company tells me how nice the microwave is, and stop to admire it, and ask me where I purchased it.

Now going up another rung, we move up the ladder to values. Personal values are an internal reference point to what is beneficial and what is not. These are imprinted on us from an early age, they can be brought about from norms of appropriateness and useful to an individual, group, and even a nation. Value, from a sales perspective are the intrinsic qualities that are brought to our attention by the sales professional. It is important to understand that values can be predictors of behavior. If you align the values of your product, with the values of your customers, this congruency helps induce a greater desire for the product by the customer. Examples of values that may be perceived as acceptable or for that matter desirable are: freedom, generosity, usefulness, trustworthiness, etc. To create a greater impact on a brand, companies elicit values that are conjoined to emotions. This creates more engagement and greater love for a product by a target or target market. Psychology has determined a correlation between excitement, an emotion, and the value fun. When buyers are excited, and the product exhibits excitement through novelty, and it is conjoined to the value of fun, there is a higher sales conversion that transpires as a result. This is, again, predictable behavior. A marketer will preframe this during the creation of promotional material, to increase the stimulus effect. At the end of the day all of these sales, marketing and branding techniques are put into place to create goodwill with the target or the target market, which builds trust. All of this works to indoctrinate the consumer to the brand, by providing goodwill, and delivering on the brand promise.

If we go back to the microwave example, we might create a brand promise as such: This brand promises to cook food in the most precise way possible, while providing the experience of modern convenience. A slogan may be phrased as: *Precise Cooking Perfect Looking!*

Now you know probably more about attributes than you ever expected to learn. The point for teaching you all of this is to make the argument for why you need to know about attributes.

We attribute value to just about everything. Values help explain why we do the things we do. With respect to religion, people value the concept of a god.

The Attribution Model holds true to two types of attributes. One is internal attributes; the other external attributes. Internal attributions are what we equate as particular internal traits people have. These are abilities, motives, and a person's overall disposition. Incidentally, Heider termed internal attribution as disposition attribution, for this reason.

People explain away their behavior through attributing it to their disposition in life; most often, when it benefits them. We have now turned away from products, and not focused on individuals, and their attributes. Just like we formulate a brand promise about a particular product or company, you can likewise do the same about an individual person.

External attribution is also called situational attribution. The reason for this is because external attributions relate to things out of our control, most often. This creates often these pseudo-cause and effect relationships. It's a false causation that happens often when people use both internal and external attribution. In my opinion this is ironic, given that when products hold certain attributes that lead to the formation of a brand promise, it usually leads to an aligned brand, because we've gone through this discovery process of determining, based on the attributes a products has, what that promise should be. When we create a brand promise for an individual, the promise is often frequently broken, because people often do not live up to these promises. This explains why some people who grew up poor, education-less, and with attributed traits that would reflect failure, can raise to the top of their professions and become extremely wealthy. The inverse of this is also true. You have people with good 'genes' who were born into wealthy families, given the best education money can buy, and yet they become failures, when everything pointed to success for them.

Often times in using language, we communicate plausibility, attributing it as causality. In other words, X causes Y. If something is plausible enough, people may very well assume it as true, and accept the suggestion. We'll touch more on this in the next chapter. I mention it here, for what I'm about to teach you next, so keep it in mind.

An external cause could be that you're going in for a job interview and the person in charge of doing the hiring, who has been asking you several questions, has asked you an open ended question, and you have confessed some flaw in your work history, for example. Maybe you've had several jobs in the past several years. This poses a red flag, for the hiring agent, because in their mind they may very well be wondering, "Well, if I hire this person, are they going to do the same thing with my company; are they going to quit this job after a few months of working for us?" After all, it is expensive training someone into a new position, only to have them quit a short while later. We are investing company money and other resources into the individual, and to have them quit is very costly! When they leave, they could very well be taking our knowledge resources and other impartations to a competitor, which can cause us even more cost.

So, imagine, if you will, that you are in this situation. Imagine you have gone through three jobs in the past year, and you're sitting there, you've been honest on your resume, and now the question comes up: "Well, you know what John, I need to ask you a couple questions about your resume that stand out as problematic. There are a couple things that concerns me. One is that you've had three jobs in the last year, and you haven't been at any of those jobs longer than three months. Quite frankly, what am I to think, and why should I assume you would work for us longer than three months?" Now, you sit before this gentleman or gentlewoman and are faced with this question. What is your answer?

Now, there could have been many reasons why you went through three jobs. Maybe you moved three times because of the promise of better opportunities or because of some family problems. Maybe one of the companies went belly-up! There are many scenarios that are plausible. Many that are excusable for why you would have gone through that many jobs. However, you have to give an answer to this person sitting across from you, and do it honestly without lying.

This takes us to attribution theory. You may say something like, "Well, you know, I know I've gone through three jobs, and I know how that must look to you, so let me please explain honestly." You're now given the opportunity. You're trying your best not to stall in your deliver. You say to this person, "The first job I had, my employer promised to give me every Sunday off, so my family and I could go to church. This was a deal breaker for me when he gave me the ultimatum that I could either skip church and time with my family to come to work, or else find work somewhere else. I knew this was illegal, but, and honestly, I didn't have the financial resources to fight this employer, and quite frankly it left a bad taste in my mouth—this experience—and so I prayed about it, and felt like quitting was the right thing to do. For the second job, I quit because my transportation broke down, and I had no public transportation option, and had no other choice but to quit. It was very unfortunate, but it was not my fault the car broke down. The last job, well, the company had hired me, but had to lay people off, and I was freshly hired, so I was the first to go. Eventually, though, the company went belly up and everybody lost their job! It was due to the troubled economy, and again, not my fault!" We'll stop here, so I can explain to you about attribution in action in this example.

If you notice, what we've done is attributed an externality (i.e., an external cause) for why we're no longer employed at any of those three jobs. Every one of the answers given, are plausible, though I'm not sure how an individual employer conducting the interview would take these excuses, but it would not be out of the realm of possibility to believe that these external causes, happened to cause the result of losing the job. The employer may even feel sorry for you! These are external events or causes that we attribute to the cause of an effect. External attribution is also referred to in psychology and persuasion circles as Fundamental Attribution; we make fundamental attributions to excuse away the effect. Most of the time when this is communicated, it is when someone wants to deflect the true cause for why something has happened to them, and, essentially place blame on something or someone outside their control, when in fact they should be pointing the finger at themselves.

On the flipside, when someone is taking credit, or praise, they generally use dispositional or internal attribution to take credit for it. For example, take our job scenario once more. You've been now hired, there working for two years, company sales are peaking, you're head of the sales department, and your boss comes over and says, "You know, one of the best decisions I ever made was hiring you. When you first sat in front of my desk, you had several things red flagging, but I went with my hunch, and my gut told me that you were the right person for this position, and my gut paid off huge dividends." Then, certainly, of course, you thank your boss, and say returning, "I think that most of the success can be attributed to my good education, my family values, and my natural ability to reason more carefully than most people." I'll once more stop, so I can explain this example.

If you notice, in this particular example, when the boss is congratulating you, he or she is praising you for doing an excellent job, but also praising himself for hiring you; doing so, less boastfully, by attributing it to his or her 'gut' or 'instincts'. These are both internal attributes and what is also called dispositional attributes. The boss is not being given, by you, an external reason for the high results produced. You're not attributing the success to the great men and women on your sales force who are excellent forces for good on your team. You're not attributing the success to the goodwill that the marketing department has created through effective promotions which have created much goodwill for the company, which has been a factor in customers wanting to buy the products. These are external attributes, but no, you want to shine like a light in the boss's eyes, and take the credit, but indirectly, through attributing the success to some aspect of yourself; an internal attribution to the success. This makes you look good, and the boss rewards you for this, benefiting you primarily. Had sales been down, and the boss was concerned, and you faced many challenges, you would have alternatively blamed something else, outside of your control, to give a plausible reason why sales quotas weren't being met. You would do this to preserve your reputation in the company, and so the boss did not think less about you as an employee or question your competencies inside your position. Don't start sweating yet, simply understand that most people, especially leaders in today's companies, do exactly this. Welcome to attribution theory!

During my undergraduate degree I took courses in interpersonal communications. This area of my program, really impacted my perspective on how attribution theory and psychological persuasion theories play such an integral role in how people interact one-on-one with one another.

Now that you know what attribution theory is all about, what you need to know, from a preacher's evaluation and application is that these types of theories, which come out of the discipline of psychology, are in fact, interdisciplinary, meaning; they cross over into preaching, just as they did my interpersonal communications course I took in college. Preachers can take and apply attribution theory likewise. You can, as a preacher, preframe ideas that are external that work against your persuasive agenda. We observe this, for example, when preachers use the metaphor of "worldliness" versus "of God". Same type of thing. We say, when someone is living a sinful existence, or not paying their tithe, that they are affected by the metaphoric disease of worldliness; that is to say, living for personal gain, as opposed to living for God, and His agenda. We blame the world, to imply subtly that it is because of living for selfishness that people do not trust God enough to provide for them what they need, which is proven because they are not paying their tenth to God. Contrariwise, as preachers, we may assert that those who do pay their tithes, are living in Godliness; as if to say, "Good people". I want to point out to you that in the Christian faith, "Goodness" or "Godliness" are values, we hold in positive high regard. There is intrinsic value in living a life for God, and some may argue also, practical value. I would, as many people who live for God, live without bad habits, like smoking cigarettes, or causing harm to others. These are practical values, though they fit into the umbrella values we hold intrinsically valuable. As a preacher, you can use these values to create persuasive arguments that can be either structured or systematic arguments or, as we've also mentioned before, heuristic, i.e. rule of thumb, arguments. As a rule of thumb we do not do anything that would have us kill another human being, nor, when you stop to think about what is involved in killing, and the punishments brought on by the society, it really is an illogical argument, that has little practical value in most situations.

Preachers can apply attribution theory, practically, by formulating persuasive arguments that either agree or counter agree with the way many people behave when applying internal and external ascriptions to their personal situations. This can be applied through storytelling, Biblical case studies, metaphors, and analogies—all done indirectly. Otherwise it can be applied directly, by building a practical case for explaining why some people blame or praise God for their situations (internal attribution); or blame their external situations for why they are moving away from a Godly standard of living (external attribution).

Respondent Conditioning Model

Respondent Conditioning is known moreover by the names of Classical Conditioning, or Pavlovian Conditioning; namely, because Ivan Pavlov is the founder of this model of psychological persuasion. Why it is important to learn is because you can use it in your preaching, to get people to respond behaviorally, by conditioning them to respond to certain provocations.

Ian Pavlov's famous experiment with dogs, and conditioning them to salivate by ringing a bell, after having rang the bell each time he fed them—even when the food wasn't given, is an example of respondent conditioning.

What applications you can use respondent conditioning for, include: anchoring your subjects to take action and give large offerings, whenever you speak in a certain tone of voice. Or, you may want to condition your subjects to get emotional whenever you speak about the teaching of Jesus, by conditioning them over time to become this way whenever you speak a certain parable.

How you may want to get people to take action is through conditioning your subjects to enter into a certain emotional state, which is associated with the state of mind people are in when they normally take a particular action or stance. How you might accomplish this would be to perfect a certain way in which you communicate that focuses your audiences full attention, then by doing something seemingly normal, such as raising your hand, or making a certain facial expression, anything really that communicates to them unconsciously without raising conscious suspicion that you are intentionally doing something weird or of concern to them. You want to make sure you set this anchor just before the peak of the emotional state you want your subjects in. After which you will then, during the peak emotional state, dismiss the anchor. In other words, if your anchor is a raised hand, you'll immediately drop it. After some time, just the raising of your hand will cause your subjects to enter into this particular emotional state.

What if you were to do this in a variety of contexts, to achieve more and more control over your subjects? Theoretically, the more you apply this persuasion tactic, the more indoctrinated your subjects would become, and the more control you would have over them. The Respondent Conditioning Model is useful for creating the True Believer phenomenon. You want your subjects over time completely trusting of you, and willing to do whatever you tell them to. Keep in mind this type of power must be used ethically and with extreme care and only for the good of the congregant. You must hold yourself accountable for the moral authority you possess.

Cognitive Dissonance Model

You have heard me mention cognitive dissonance throughout this first chapter, already, and you understand by now that one way to look at cognitive dissonance is to think of it as buyer's remorse, which you know is when a customer regrets buying something after a purchase has been made, and now you know I'll be teaching you how you can apply this model of persuasion so your preaching is much more effective. Why you need to know what cognitive dissonance is, and how to apply it to your preaching, is because cognitive dissonance deals directly with the core of cognition concepts; namely: thoughts, beliefs, and attitudes. It is fairly easy to size up what people want, of course; especially when you know what they want to avoid and seek to attract into their lives. Let's learn more...

What exactly is cognitive dissonance? This persuasion theory was coined in 1956 by Leon Festinger. The word cognitive was explained by Festinger, in his book, *A Theory of Cognitive Dissonance*, as:

"The terms "dissonance" and "consonance" refer to relations which exist between pairs of "elements." It is consequently necessary, before proceeding to define these relations, to define the elements themselves as well as we can.

"These elements refer to what has been called cognition, that is, the things a person knows about himself, about his behavior, and about his surroundings. These elements, then, are "knowledges," if I may coin the plural form of the word. Some of these elements represent knowledge about oneself: what one does, what one feels, what one wans or desires, what one is and the like. Other elements of knowledge concern the world in which one lives: what is where, what leads to what, what things are satisfying or painful or inconsequential or important, etc.

"It is clear that the term "knowledge" has been used to include things to which the word does not ordinarily refer—for example, opinions. "A person does not hold an opinion unless he thinks it is correct, and so, psychologically, it is not different from a "knowledge." The same is true of beliefs, values, or attitudes, which function as "knowledges" for our purposes."

The essence, we gather, is that cognition are our thoughts, beliefs, and attitudes. Mentioned in these are opinions, and values. I personally like the adoption of the word "knowledges" in which Festinger uses to capture all these elements of cognition.

Dissonance is psychological discomfort caused when two or more cognitions converge which are not in consonance, i.e. agreement. You might want to think of it as psychological pain, caused as a result of belief conflicts.

Festinger put forward the idea that whenever cognitive dissonance occurs, we are motivated to reduce the dissonance until mental balance is restored. One experiment the Festinger as a part of, which you might find interesting, is an experiment in which people were asked to do a very boring, mundane task. The participants were either paid $1 or $20 to complete this task, which took only an hour. When one group finished the boring assignment, and another group was brought in to do it, the previous group was instructed to tell the next group that the assignment was fun and exciting. The result of the experiment yielded that those paid $20 did not do as good a job of convincing those paid only a dollar that the task was fun and exciting. The reason behind this phenomenon had to do with the lack of dissonance occurring in those paid $20, versus the dissonance which happened in those paid only a dollar. Reason would have it that a boring task should pay better than a dollar. For this reason, the participants, to eliminate this cognitive dissonance, had to change their beliefs that the task was exciting and fun, so convince themselves that it was worth doing for a dollar. Those who were paid $20, did not experience dissonance, so they could be honest and forthright and share that the experience was actually boring.

When I was seventeen there was an elderly neighbor who called me over to his house one afternoon, after school. He asked me to mow his yard, as he claimed he was too old to push a push-mower. He told me upfront, that if I helped him, he would reward me well for my helping him.

It was an extremely large yard, having both a front and back yard, and much space on the sides as well. After I finished, I cleaned his lawn mower, and was taking it to his garage. The man, keep in mind, lived in a very stately home, and I assumed, like most might, that he was wealthy. Before, I could put the lawn mower back, he asked me to use a leaf blower to blow the lawn clippings from off his yard. He wanted it to look perfect he told me. Though I was extremely tired, having taken me several hours to mow, I did not try and reason with him, but did as he requested.

When I finished, it was nearly all the way dark outside; I smelt like grass, itched, my shoes were badly stained, and I had not even begun on the homework I needed to complete. I felt stressed thinking about how late I'd be up and how little sleep I would get before having to get up and catch the school bus.

How do we use this model of cognitive dissonance to make our preaching more persuasive? You might be asking this very question, now, inside your mind? This is a valid question, and so I'll give you some steps to take so you'll know one way you can apply this theory. With a little more thought, you'll be able to come up with more ways, certainly, and I'll leave that up to you to do.

I. **Step 1**. Start with the end in mind. This means decide what your main objective is, and then look at what responses you want your subjects to experience and take away from your message. If you want your audience to feel excited and on fire for Jesus, you start here.

II. **Step 2**. Craft a message that will require an investment from your audience. Provide value in your message, however, be sure to charge more than what your value is valued at. You'll have to use your good sense to do this.

III. **Step 3**. Promote your message's value, to gain your subjects attention; making sure to incite interest and desire.

IV. **Step 4**. Charge for your message. This doesn't mean you have to ask for money upfront, or that you have to make a ridiculous demand on your audience. In the context of preaching, it simply means gaining some form of compliance from your audience. Get some form of action, which you want.

V. **Step 5**. Deliver your message. Give full value.

VI. **Step 6**. Before you are finished, ask for what you really want. Make sure this happens before you really deliver the best value. In other words: save the best for last, and only deliver when you have received what you wanted.

In the example of wanting your message to create an internal motivation in your subjects to get on fire for Jesus, this is the action or price tag you're requiring before you deliver the true value of your message. What happens psychologically is your audience feels vested in your sermon, and this investment creates expectation. Even if your sermon doesn't deliver the value they internally expect, they will, because of the cognitive dissonance happening, perceive it as the ultimate value, because they do not want to feel discomfort from having invested something. They will also take your message, and share it with others, creating more of a cult-like following for your ministry.

The goodwill that gets created as a result of this approach to message delivery helps elevate you on a pedestal, and encourages more future investment from your subjects. They will walk away feeling on fire for Jesus, and they will look forward to attending your services. This is a great way of indoctrinating people into the body of Christ.

The main thing to remember when it comes to the Cognitive Dissonance Model is people will do one of four things usually in response to dissonance:

I.   **One**, change their minds about one of the aspects of their cognitive perception (e.g., quit attending your preaching).

II.   **Two**, reduce the importance of a thought cognition (e.g., reduce the importance of the cost).

III.   **Three**, increase the overlay concerning the two; meaning, the subject convinces him or herself that the message being preached is more valuable than it actually is.

IV.   **Four**, take a different look at the cost versus reward; meaning, the subject, through re-evaluation, sees the reward of the preaching, valued at more than the cost (increasing the intrinsic value).

Elaboration Likelihood Model

This model of persuasion is similar to where we started when we covered the structural-heuristic case study of Chaiken. This model was created by Richard E. Petty and John Cacioppo back during the 1980s when Chaiken was conducting her persuasion experiment. Petty and Cacioppo came up with two routes by which subject's change attitudes and become persuaded. The first route is the central route, similar to Chaiken's structural processing theory; where subjects process information more central to them based on the pros and cons of the persuasive argument. This requires effective communication that can elicit relevant mental representations, called elaboration likelihood. The other route is the peripheral route, and entails bypassing deliberation processing, a function of the central route; so that subjects are persuaded based on the source of the communication.

Why it is important to understand both of these routes to persuasion through the mental likelihood that the subject will elaborate mentally on a particular message is because it goes back to the heart of persuasion in general. When someone is motivated and paying attention, they tend to take the central route to decision-making. This means they adopt a more logical approach to considering ideas. When someone has less mental ability to focus the tendency is for them to make decisions based peripheral cues; such as, what the speaker looks like, how much rapport they have with the subject, and how well the persuasive message is delivered with regard to surface characteristics.

What you really need to understand is that when people process information more logically, and become persuaded by ideas presented, they generally change their mind for a longer period of time. When people are persuaded by the peripheral route, change may not be near as long; however, swaying someone to adopt an idea or take a particular action may be faster coming and relevant in the short term. As a persuasion artist you need to consider your agenda. If your agenda is for the subject to weigh the pros and cons in order to make a truly informed decision about whether an idea or action is right for them and their mental makeup then the central route is your best option. If, on the other hand, you want someone to adopt an idea quickly and to take action, though they may later change their opinion, then the peripheral route is your best option.

When I was in private practice as a hypnotherapist, hypnotizing clients to stop smoking for example, half the persuasion battle was won when the client decided to become hypnotized. This is because they had already weighed, using the central route, the pros and cons of stopping smoking. The route of persuasion I took in my hypnosis session with them was more or less the peripheral route; namely, because all that was required was for them to focus their attention on something I would have them focus on, and then for them to bypass their critical faculty, i.e. bypassing the deliberation process, so that they would just accept my hypnotic suggestions. In this case, I utilized a dual approach, where I let the subject weigh out the pros and cons of smoking in their mind; coming to terms with it. Then I reinforced this with low elaboration, more hypnotic, peripheral routes to helping them create quick changes, which were backed by their more high level, more central and conscious beliefs.

How to apply the elaboration likelihood model will require you to first consider if your subject requires a high elaboration; meaning, a high degree of mental elaboration to ensure that they change their mind and accept your message on a more permanent basis, or whether low elaboration is all that is required. One decision is more a logical, conscious decision. The other, i.e. peripheral, is less logical and more unconscious processing. Once you have considered what is required, you can then either structure a sound logical argument, or else work on your appearance and rapport building skills to ensure that the subject complies with the message or suggestion you are presenting them with.

Functional Model

In schools of Psychology, Functionalism is attributed to its founding by the Father of American Psychology, William James. The fundamentals of functionalism shift us away from the earlier ideas of Structuralism, and take us into a whole new world altogether. Whereas structuralism dealt with more the idea of mental consciousness, functionalism takes us into a more pragmatic use of psychology; as it applies to understanding divergent attitudes an individual may have toward other people, objects, or even issues, when placed in certain situations and environments.

Why you need to understand functionalism is because it provides us with more a basis of how persuasion can be used to achieve functional results, through experimentation, testing, and measurement. This shift to functionalism from structuralism during psychology's history, paves the way in opening the door to understanding behaviors and why people do what they do, and how they react to what they do. Understanding the function of behavior provides us with more obvious understanding into predictive behavior.

What you need to understand about functionalism are the four main functional attitudes:

I.   Adjustment Function is the first, and is the idea that people will be motivated to increase positive external rewards, while minimizing the costs. We see this all the time when people are making purchases. They want the house, but don't want to pay for it, or, at the very least; don't want to pay much for it. People want a deal!

II.   Ego Defensive Function is the second. This is a situation where someone might want to protect themselves from themselves. In other words this function of behavior happens when someone is threatened by their own negative impulses or bad thoughts. When I was in India, I met a man, who heard someone criticize their inability to pass their school exams. The man I met instantly put his hands over his ears so the man would stop. Then he said, "My god man, do not talk like this, your thoughts are powerful, and you will fail if you keep talking. Never talk like that, okay!?" This was an example of ego defensiveness in action.

III. The third functional attitude is Value-Expressive. This is when someone wants to remain congruent with their self-concept or image of themselves and so they will "play the part" so to speak to live up to their mental representation and beliefs about who they want to be characterized as. I have a friend who is an adjunct professor at a small university, and he wears black tee-shirts and a blazer over his khakis, displaying himself as an intellectual; this is, the mental representation he has of himself. He looks definitely like a college professor, and carries himself in this form.

IV. The last is the Knowledge Function, and this attitude type revolves around a person who may want to gain knowledge to achieve a sense of control over their life. The adopted attitudes are chosen to set in place standards and their sense of being.

What's of dominant importance, with regard to these attitudes, are the persuasiveness of a message when directed towards a particular attitude function, as how persuasive the message is, will to a large extent, determine if someone changes their mind or not and adopt the new attitude. Therapists understand this function of psychological attitudes to some extent; understanding that when a client comes in with a problem of depression or anxiety, and their attitude is reflective of the state they are in, will challenge (e.g., provocative therapy, etc.) in order for the subject to make a change in attitude to come out of their state of mind that is not useful to them anymore. The subject simply needs to accept the idea that their attitude is not as useful as another attitude, and change can happen more easily.

How do we apply all this to our preaching? The answer lies in the ability to shift attitudes, by recognizing different people's identification with a particular one of the four attitude functionalities. All you have to really do is recognize where someone is at, then focus your persuasive message in a way that will be most useful for affecting changes within the individual. In a group setting you may need to cater to various attitudes in ways that will overall affect the group.

Inoculation Model

The inoculation model is observed often times in the media and advertising; especially, when it comes to politicking. A candidate may be running for an office, with a less than perfect character. The campaign may minimize this by creating a marketing campaign that exposes it in a lesser light, than it truly should be displayed. When the opposing party puts forward another character-killing fact, the audience will dismiss it, associating it to the original message that was put out, thinking that the rivalry is just over exaggerating the issue.

The reverse of this can be true as well. It could be that a company wants to make a rival company appear to be liars with flawed promises about a particular product. Company 'A' puts forward an blatant lie that was advertised by company 'B' and when consumers see the ads of company 'B' they assume everything they are saying is nothing more than a lie, and therefore dismiss this company as a company they want to do business with.

How you can use it in your preaching ministry is by inoculating obvious flaws in how people in other religions say one thing, yet do another, of course; which in turn will have your congregation believing you more and dismissing that other religious belief system even more. Many of the most effective preachers I have worked with have used this model to reinforce loyalty to their own preaching ministry, while discouraging open-mindedness to any other popular religion or belief system.

I have a relative who attends church several times per week. He heard his pastor deliver a remark about a politician who he claimed was responsible for donating millions of dollars to Muslim organizations. This inoculated a belief in my relative to where he began to hate Muslims and a particular political party, while reinforcing how much he loved his church and the pastor. One evening, chatting over Skype messenger, he relayed this message to me, in an attempt to win me to his way of thinking. I excused myself for five minutes, citing I needed to do something, and checked the facts of this online, and discovered that though the politician was only partially responsible for donating this money to ancient historical reconstruction projects of mosques, in fact, even more money was allocated to rebuilding and refurbishing churches, Hindu temples, and other historical buildings. The context was not a religious propagation for Islam; rather, it was to preserve ancient historical sites, many of which were not even in use anymore. Interestingly, most of the allocated budget went to preserving Christian churches. The real propagation happening was by the pastor inoculating these ideas in his persuasive messages to influence his congregation to despise other religions, and a particular political party, which he disagreed with. It had nothing to do with Jesus and Christianity, per se.

Narrative Transportation Model

You really need to pay attention to this particular model. We'll be revisiting it again, in future chapters, so keep it in mind. Storytelling is one of the earliest forms of communication, primitive humans engaged in to impart information. We see evidence of this in early cave paintings were primitive people drew on cave walls the history of things which happened, so they would not be forgotten. It is interesting actually to look at these cave drawings and try and imagine what life must have been like way back then in history. Imagining what life must have been like, we formulate mental pictures, attitudes, and certain intentions about what life would have been like. We can even picture ourselves in their shoes and relate from our own perspectives. In essence we're being transported into the narrative where we lose ourselves, and mentally we change, and even become entirely different people. Of course it's just a story right? Real life, you might argue, is more than a story, am I right? Don't think about it too long, you might change your own mind. Stories are very hypnotic and great tools for changing minds.

Why do you need to learn about Narrative Transportation Model? You need to learn about it, because, in my experience, having worked with some of the most incredibly persuasive preachers and presenters, stories were the number one tool used to persuade someone to change their mind, and adopt a desired behavior or action. In my opinion stories make the mind malleable. In this way, reality becomes plastic and ideas and persuasive messages can create a real impact on your subject's belief system.

What you may want to take away from the Narrative Transportation Model is that when someone enters a narrative, they, because of empathy to the characters, change their intentions and attitudes, to reflect those of the characters. We in essence, take on the life of the characters.

How you can use stories to persuade others is by reciting stories to create a sense of transportation from the reality of origin, into the false reality of the story. People often times lose themselves so deep in a story, using their imagination and faculties of pretend, that they actually lose touch with the reality of origin, and enter a brand new reality. When it comes to persuasion and recounting the lessons of history, nothing in my opinion is less innocent than a story. When people enter a story, they are partially not present in the reality of origin; namely, because they are engaged attention-wise in the story. This creates a here and there effect. You can be in one place, and yet in another, creating a sense of two realities. Some people may understand this concept better by looking at it in the context of a dream world and an everyday reality. To those who have dreamt, a dream can seem very real indeed. The same holds true of a story.

What if you created some stories to add to your preaching? Do you think that you could more easily shift attitudes? What about making people stop and think and introspect on what it is you're advocating? Do you think they would get your message easier? I think so. I think if you start applying and learning how to tell better stories, you preaching will be so much more impacted positively that you'll surprise yourself will all the many ways you can use narratives to change minds and persuade your sheep to follow you down any road you wish. Narrative Transportation relies on empathy with the characters and mental imagery with causes them to suspend reality and the story plot activates an individual's imagination. When you are able to suspend your subject's reality, you are able to elsewise suspend their disbeliefs; opening them to accept whatever you desire for them to accept.

Social Judgment Model

The Social Judgment Model was developed by Carolyn Sherif, Muzafer Sherif and Carl Hovland. This social judgement model has really three parts to it. The first part is we make decisions in terms of what we perceive as true, and which we'll get on board with, from this acceptance latitude. This acceptance latitude you can envision as a target. You're getting ready to shoot an arrow toward, on an archer's range. What you can think of, is you've got this center area of the target, a red area, which some people label a bull's eye, yet, we'll just call an area of acceptance in which if you fire off a message, it is the likelihood that an individual will accept that message or not.

We have another ring, just outside the bull's eye, which is the area of indifference and this area of indifference is actually latitude of non-commitment or latitude of indifference. If you go outside this area of the target, we have another circle, which is more on the outside of the target which we have labeled the latitude of rejection. Essentially, if you can envision these then you can get a good sense of what social judgment theory is all about.

When someone is being presented a persuasive message, i.e. persuasive argument, that is to say; they typically will sort out the message subconsciously from the attitude in which their currently in. They do this naturally, and it sort of happens that when they do this, they will decide if this is something I instantly accept, is it something I am indifferent towards, or is it something I flat-out reject automatically.

An interesting thing happens in sales. Sales of course is a very persuasive field or occupation, and what happens is a sale's professional will walk into an environment and not really know what that environment is. It could be that you're walking into a small business, and maybe they put in windshields in people's cars. So they specialize in glass cutting and all that entails. Maybe you go up to the business owner and they are friendly toward you, and inviting. You begin to get into why you're there, and what you have to present to them. As a result the person makes a decision yes or no to buy your product. In the process of making the decision, depending on how well you associate your message with in alignment or congruence with their attitude, will determine whether or not you are going to make that sale or not.

Sales professionals have learned this the hard way getting started, while some may have a sixth-sense and be able to intuit when presenting a message and if it will be effective or not, do determine if they should proceed or come back later to present. It is sort of an intuitive, unconscious, subconscious, other mind, means adopted for knowing when to present a persuasive message.

So the real reason you need to understand this is because when you're presenting a message in your preaching, there are going to be some people who flat-out reject the message, some who are indifferent to the message, and others who receptive and accepting and you're greatest advocate and they are going to accept that everything you say is the Gospel.

How do we get people on board, and start to accept ideas, a little bit at a time. How do we actually start to get people to embrace our ideas, i.e. our ideologies, so that we can indoctrinate them into a different philosophy, argument, so that they get on board, start to take action, start to believe us, become more in rapport and alignment with our message, and become an advocate for our cause? So how do we do all of this? Well, that's a great question! What we do is start to observe that there are certain anchor points, and the anchor points are actually the point, right dab in the middle, of our acceptance circle, i.e. what in psychology we call the latitude of acceptance, and this critical point is the point of the ideal state of mind, the ideal attitude a person will have to where when we tell them something, so long as it is aligned with them unconsciously, they, for the most part, will accept it right out of the gate.

How do we actually get people to accept ideas, maybe, that are a little outside the latitude of acceptance; perhaps on the border of the latitude of indifference? Well, if we are presenting an idea, the first step you want to do is understand the individual or the group of people that you are going to be preaching to, so that you can start to formulate a structure in which you can start to adjust people's anchor point, to bring it closer to the attitude necessary for them to accept your ideas. There is a process for doing this, which we'll cover now.

The process begins with step 1, we judge how close or how far away a particular person's position from our argument actually is. We get a sense by knowing our audience. We can do this intuitively by asking question, or feeling out the situation, and knowing more and more through the process of learning and taking in information about our group, what their ideas and philosophies are. Chances are if you've been a preacher over a congregation for any period of time you're beginning to get certain cues about to let you know exactly where that set-point or anchor point is for your congregation.

The next step, step 2, is to shift their position in response to the argument we're making. This is done, for example, when we realize someone adjusts their attitude whenever they start to judge a new position; their latitude of acceptance, that bull's eye area, if you will. Now someone starts to judge that a message is in their rejection zone, i.e. their latitude of rejection. In this case they are also going to shift their attitude as well, but toward the polar opposite direction of where we want them to.

One of the notions, these researchers discovered, was that often times when a message is presented, and it is in the zone of acceptance, but more towards the periphery of acceptance, close to the latitude of indifference, that when they accept a message they accept it from a stronger position than what they, under other circumstances likely would, and it actually becomes a stronger perception of attitude for them than it would have become otherwise. The same holds true with the rejection zone. If someone is on the periphery of rejection, nearer towards the indifference zone, if they perceive it as rejection, then it becomes a strong attitude of rejection.

When a sales professional is out there in the field selling a particular product they run into resistance, or they run into complete acceptance of the presentation; selling whatever it is they're pushing. They get someone right out of the gates rejecting whatever they are presenting – there's a strong probability the individual will reject everything, due to this. If we can get someone, on the other hand, to accept some of our ideas and agree with us in some respect, the individual's attitude will start to shift towards that anchor point, and then when we present something more in the outlaying periphery, nearer to the indifference zone, the message will be accepted, and strongly accepted, in the same way a message closer to the anchor point would have.

To change a person's attitude toward ones proposition requires us to gain an agreement set, or yes-set from them from the outset of the interaction. A simple yes-set could, for example, be agreeing about something commonly accepted fact, and then we would be able to present ideas are plausible, though less near to the anchor, and the same quality of agreement will happen naturally.

On the flip side, the inverse applies as well. For example, if you start to relay information that people outright reject, then if you do get something plausible or nearly spot-on in terms of why most people would agree to it, these individuals will be tainted from the get-go and reject even these persuasions. Keep in mind the unconscious or subconscious processing plays a critical role in this particular model of persuasion. This is very important, because people make decision based on their attitudes, beliefs, opinions, and values –and, a lot of this has to do with state of mind. So if someone is in the wrong state of mind, and they're not in a buying state necessarily, and you're trying to persuade them, you're going to have a difficult time getting them to buy what you're selling. Anything you try and sell them will be perceived as "out-there" in the latitude of rejection zone. Even if it is in the latitude of indifference, it still will be cast out and rejected, most likely. The key thing to remember is to change a person's state of mind, attitudes about you and your communications, and have them perceive you as agreeable with them, so that they will be agreeable towards you as well. You want them to believe you, and trust you, and so all of these types of factors matter. All of this is done at first on the unconscious level of communication, and the non-verbal level (e.g., body language, facial expressions, etc.). So keep all of this in mind.

How this applies to preaching is perhaps more indirect in nature. You'll want to present yourself as agreeable, in alignment from the start with their values, beliefs, and etc. so that they are immediately agreeing with you. Then you can present ideas which are plausible or far from plausible, and, because you have unconscious agreement already, when you preach your message, you want to get through, you'll have less resistance, and more success functionally achieving your end result.

What if you take this and apply it as well to your other areas of communication. You can essentially be practicing all of these models when the need arises for you to apply one over another, etc. You'll be honing your skills, increasing your effectiveness as a persuader, and ensuring that you're getting more of what you want and less of what you don't want.

One time I was asked to preach in front of a large congregation, on the way to a church I was invited to visit. I had absolutely nothing prepared, and not much experience preaching, and did my absolute best to refuse, and in the end, applying only this particular model of persuasion, gained an agreement set right off the bat with the congregation, and delivered a very persuasive message, from a few scriptures I memorized on the ride to church. At the end of the sermon, I was congratulated, and asked by many people to please return for the evening service to preach as well. The preacher was also impressed with my preaching and how absorbed his congregants were in my preaching. I shrugged all of these compliments off to the idea that they were probably excited to be hearing a fresh voice and because it was something new, they hadn't experienced before, it was a phenomenon that happens much like when a child receives a new toy. They are engaged in the toy for a short period of time, before they embrace another toy that enters their reality.

How to Apply Persuasion Models?

We've learned what the models of persuasion are now let's learn how to apply these to our preaching. Fascinatingly, I have seen these models used by some of the most persuasive preachers in a world use them in two ways. Firstly, I have seen them explained (not using the names of the models; rather, the principles) to relate a point with the audience to actually have the audience influence themselves or think about how they've been persuaded by the Devil. Secondly, I have seen them used on the audience of subjects to literally persuade the audience to be persuaded by the preacher's message. This is where the preacher would take the principles of these models and use them to persuade his or her audience.

This repurposing of these models to explain away what the audience needs to be careful to avoid actually helps to build rapport with the audience; rather, so when the preacher uses the models on his or her audience they will not be aware they are being used on them—for example, a preacher may cite how people are affected by narrative transportation; that is, told a lie inside a story, that takes them away from God and drops them into the fiery pits of Hell. Then the preacher may tell a different story to persuade the subjects to become overwhelmed by religious persuasions and have them donating money to a mission project or something altogether different. The point is both methods of applying these models is used to perfection by the best preachers.

How you apply these various persuasion models is by application and practice. At the end of this chapter there will be a number of action steps which will help you specifically apply these models into your preaching.

What if You Apply Persuasion Models?

If you apply these persuasion models and theories you'll discover an immediate shift and greater flexibility in how you are able to deliver a sermon and how you preach in general.

If you study this chapter and start to study people, you'll become aware of how often people unconsciously apply these models of persuasion and theories all the time when they interact with others. These models and theories of persuasion were, after all, discovered by studying human behavior, tendencies, and doing much research in the fields of persuasion psychology.

If you want to get creative you may want to study other people for the benefit of modeling them and borrowing their unique adaptations and techniques of these models. When you see these models of persuasion being used it is a good idea to take note of so you can utilize the same approach if you find it effectively works.

Chapter Summary

As you can tell by now, persuasion is a broad area of psychology. During the times of Socrates, rhetoric and question based selling was important for winning cases in courts of law. The person able to communicate most effectively, essentially won the argument being debated. In a time, when you were presumed guilty, until which time you could be proven innocent, proving innocence was masterfully accomplished through rhetoric and various persuasion tactics, involving something so simply as asking a mere question. This is one reason, in this first chapter, I mention the question asked by Jesus to Saul.

We've covered a lot of ground, good ground, of course; good ground for helping you to become a more persuasive communicator. I believe in my personal opinion that understanding these models of persuasion are important for laying the bedrock of various persuasion and influence tactics we'll be covering within this book. This is a reason for the long length of this first chapter. Do not be frightened with this long chapter. I could have easily broken this chapter into three distinct chapters alone (e.g., what is persuasion, persuasion theories and history, and persuasion models). I decided a better use of our time would be to combine all of this into a single chapter, so you could get a purview of persuasion from the start; namely, to be able to build upon a foundation so you could quickly become masterful of all the lessons contained in this book. When we cover various tactics, you'll already know, consciously or unconsciously, why you need to know what I'm teaching, what it will do for you and your ministry, and how you can adopt it strategically to get the best results. You'll also be able to ask yourself, through introspection, what would happen if you applied it in a different manner, to intuit what your results might look like.

Persuasion is an umbrella term for influence. Essentially what I want you to get out of this first chapter is the various persuasion models that have been previously tested and conceived by psychologists, in which you can also test and determine their effectiveness, by practically applying them in the ways I've suggested you - them.

I want to recap, now, before I finish off this chapter, by going back through and highlighting some of the main points we've covered, to give you an overview of everything we've covered thus far.

We first started out talking about the importance of language. I mentioned how language itself can help us to be more persuasive. I've covered the fundamentals of persuasion which is simply to affect changes in someone's beliefs, attitudes, intentions, motivations, and behaviors. You've learned how to be more persuasive using various models. You've learned how people organize and conceptualize ideas in order to sell themselves mentally on our ideas and propositions.

In the beginning we looked at the systematic persuasion theory which is a nice way of saying they are going to structurally organize our persuasive argument in their mind, and weigh the pros and cons. They will do this to make a consciously informed decision. This conscious effort requires more mental energy and effort on the subject's part, which can be draining psychologically. It requires processing information step-by-step, in order for them to make an informed decision and believe our argument or not. Keep in mind, the more drained someone is, the more susceptible they are to receiving unconscious messages, as their critical faculty or ability to break down the deliberation process starts to erode, allowing them to suspend their disbelief and more easily accept anything as the truth, i.e. accepting our persuasions.

We next turned our attention to heuristic persuasion. The heuristic model, Chaiken developed, gives us more the unconscious cues that people use in order to make quicker, on-the-spot, decisions. These decisions may not be as long lasting or as long term as some persuasion messages would need to be. If we're winning someone into the Christian fold, for example, for the purpose of indoctrination of the Christian philosophy, then a structural approach would be better used to serve the purpose, as we want lifetime Christians. If we're talking about something not so necessarily long lasting, perhaps it is about various persuasions in church doctrine and actions to help bring more people to Christ Jesus, we might consider using a more heuristic approach. We could, for example, if we want members to tithe or donate money to a mission outreach, or revival preach to take up as a love offering, then the type of message would be better served using a heurist approach. It would only be necessary to convince people to give one time for a love offering for example.

Next we discussed various persuasion models. We started with Attribution Model. Explaining how dispositional/internal attribution and situational/external attribution. I've given you the difference, by sharing how dispositional/internal attribution is when we attribute our inner qualities and personal features are used primarily in contexts where we want to take credit for something that benefits us positively, and where with situational/external attributions we give primarily when an excuse is needed to offset personal responsibility. When someone is wishing to explain why they were unable to fulfill some type of obligation, they are more likely to give an external attribution (e.g., my dog ate my homework analogy), but when they are credited with something being positively attributed to them they may cite some internal attribute (e.g., I've always had an internal drive to be excellent in all situations.).

The next model we discussed was the Respondent Conditioning Model. This model, also called Classical conditioning, or Pavlovian conditioning, is what happens when we condition someone to react whenever a particular stimuli is present. This is also called an anchored response. An example is when someone recalls a memory from their past, when they are confronted with an external stimuli, such as a certain location. When the subject revisits a local park, they may instantly recall a memory from childhood, experiencing mentally all that they experienced during that childhood event. In psychology, Ivan Pavlov, did experiments with dogs; where he conditioned them to salivate and expect food whenever they heard a tuning fork sound. This was accomplished by feeding them a small snack, and ringing a bell. Overtime, the sound of the bell/tuning fork was all that was required for the dogs to expect and start salivating for the food. Preachers can apply this model to their preaching using stage presence, tone of voice, a particular suit worn, and so on, to put their audience into a particular state of mind, or to prepare them for a particular message in which they are conditioned unconsciously to accept and comply with.

The next model we covered was the Cognitive Dissonance Model. This model, developed by Leon Festinger, in effect, concludes that whenever someone is faced with dissonance they are going to respond in one of four ways to alleviate the dissonance: (a) change mind about their mental state, (b) reduce cognitive importance, (c) increase the overlap between the two, and (d) look at the cost/reward ration and revaluate it. These four methods apply to the buyer's remorse a buyer experiences when purchasing a new car. The buyer can alleviate cognitive dissonance, i.e. buyer's remorse in one of four ways: (a) return the car, (b) reduce the importance of the money spent, (c) convince self that he/she was not taken advantage of, and (d) re-evaluate the purchase, and rationalize logically that the car is more valuable than the money spent to purchase it and perhaps it is a necessity. Preachers can apply these four methods to sell their persuasive message to their audience, to better help their congregants accept that what the preacher is asking them to do is more valuable than what he/she is asking them to give up, etc.

The next model covered was the Functional Theories Model. This model included the adjustment function, ego defensive function, value-expressive function, and knowledge function. In the main, each function describes how external attitudes mask internal beliefs, yet, exhibit a "tell" that might reflect that internal belief. People, for example will buy both utilitarian and personal identity products and have certain attitudes that match each. Advertisers will adopt a message that matches the attitudes buyers will have, as an appeal to that individuals self-identity for self-identity products (e.g., perfume, a reflection of one's self-identity) or utilitarian needs fulfillment with a utilitarian product (e.g., coffee maker, a reflection of utility). A person's attitude toward a stimulus may show signs of evidence regarding that individual's internal beliefs. Once the beliefs are determined it is achievable to customize messages to alter those beliefs; thus changing attitudes.

Adjustment function is where individuals are motivated to increase external rewards while minimizing the costs of those rewards. The attitude one may present will serve to direct behavior toward what is valuable while having them stray away from what is costly.

Ego Defensive function is where individuals protect themselves from their own negative thoughts about themselves, and their attitudes reflect protectionism around their own egos. A sales professional may want to stay away from exhibiting an attitude of defeat and negativity, while protecting their ego by displaying instead an attitude of strong self-confidence. It is possible to consider their internal beliefs about themselves, by understanding the function of ego defensiveness. Once understood, the person persuading them, may utilize this fear of defeat to change their attitude altogether, perhaps helping them to feel more accomplished about this aspect of their life. In turn, their attitude will change to reflect a new internal belief about themselves.

Value-expressive function is when an individual gets a pleasure from displaying themselves in alignment with their self-concept of who they believe themselves to be. We can view the attitude that comes with the self-representation to reflect their internal beliefs. If we alter those beliefs through the delivery of persuasive messages, we will see a change in how they outwardly present themselves, letting us know that an internal change in self-concept has occurred.

Knowledge function is when an individual needs to feel like they have control and understanding over their life, and therefore their attitude will reflect certain standards and rules they have for governing their activities. Observing these sets of attitudes by direct observation methods, an influence artist may recognize exactly what those internal beliefs are that this individual holds in high regard and low regard. Beliefs can therefore be changed through complying with the rules, and making shifts in the individual's rule-structure over time.

The next model we studied was the Inoculation Model. This model is where a thought is presented in a weaker or stronger form to either credit or discredit an individual or group. Others will refute other posits by the group, after taking note of a former idea being false; in which case, one negative reduces all positives to a negative perception, thus discrediting the individual or group. This is in alignment with the idea that it takes a lifetime to build character, but only takes one negative event to eradicate a person's character. From a preaching context, preachers only need to seed an idea about a particular group or individual to either insinuate a positive characterization or negative characterization about the individual or group. Nothing that the group or individual says after the negative or positive seed has been put in place can affect the initial perception of the congregants; generally speaking, that is.

The next model we took notice of was the Narrative Transportation Model. This model brings to light how individuals are swept away in a story, in which their empathy for the characters and involvement in the plot lets them change their attitudes, values, beliefs, and mental states, to reflect those within the narrative. Stories are a powerful mechanism for creating an environment in which change is possible and lasting through one's ability to imagine new realities and possibilities.

> "I am enough of an artist to draw freely upon my imagination. Imagination is more important than knowledge. Knowledge is limited. Imagination encircles the world."
>
> —Albert Einstein

The next model we learned about was the Social Judgment Model. This model is when individuals subconsciously sort and respond to a persuasive message based around the anchor point or immediate attitude they possess. When the message comes at them, they sort it unconsciously, and compare it to their current attitude, and the persuasion gets filed into one of three latitudes; namely: (a) latitude of acceptance, (b) latitude of indifference or non-commitment, or (c) latitude of rejection. This filing determines the likelihood someone will comply with accepting a persuasion and behave accordingly or not. To change the anchor point, centered in the latitude of acceptance, requires changing the person's attitude, to change the likelihood that they will accept the persuasion. The size of each latitude will vary greatly based on how we perceive that idea coming at us as relevant to our own passions, beliefs, and how we perceive ourselves.

To increase the likelihood of acceptance of a persuasive message, preachers can apply aspects of a in individual's or group's most closely accepted values and passions and weave these into the message to increase the likelihood they fall within the group's or individual's latitude of acceptance. We observe this happening during election years, when we notice a candidate acting and conveying a particular adaptation of a message to appeal to a constituent's ideals and egoistic desires. Preachers can do the same; especially, when preaching in different locations, where values and importance will vary widely away from their home church.

Action Steps

The following actions steps are meant to help you bridge the great divide from theory to action. I've heard it said that 80% of self-help books never get read all the way through, and only 20% of people ever complete the action steps found at the end of each chapter. Maybe you've heard of the 80/20 rule:

> *"So the 80/20 Principle states that there in an inbuilt imbalance between causes and results, inputs and outputs, and effort and reward."*
>
> —*Richard Koch*

In other words, 80% of the wealth winds up in the hands of 20% of the population. Twenty percent of products contribute to eighty percent of sales. This statistical discovery has been labeled Pareto's Law, after its founder, Italian economist, Vilfredo Pareto. Pareto in 1906 discovered that 80% of Italy's land was owned by 20% of the population. Significantly, this is found in economics, business, and many other disciplines to ring true; where 20% of some group will benefit from the efforts of the other 80% of the population of that group. These imbalances create leveraged opportunities for those willing to capitalize and do what the 20% does, while avoiding what the 80% doesn't do. I'm sure you can relate this back to one of our persuasion models if you go looking for it.

Suffice to say, I want you to be in the 20% of action takers and gain the true value of what I have to teach you. Certainly the choice is yours, and I'm not there to strike the back of your hands with a rule-stick; however, should you decide to pursue the true value, you'll gain the most, and realize the rewards that 80% percent of the readers won't. Not everyone will be truly great—will you?

I will be repeating this exact same intro to the action steps for each chapter. Do not be alarmed and think I'm doing it on accident to fill up pages. If I wanted to fill up pages, I'd increase the font size and double-space the lines, and add in a bunch of filler; I wouldn't do that to you! Remember back and recall the first words of this chapter:

"Only what we keep hearing do we believe."

—Bryan Westra

I.   Recognize how you are persuaded. Create a short summary of which models make the most sense to you, and which have you been persuaded by, whenever someone had attempted to apply the principles of that particular model.

II.   Write out your favorite models and the verbiage that is most attractive to you from this first chapter. Create an action plan on paper, which you will use immediately to persuade someone to take some action. As you are persuading them, watch their non-verbal behavior, and the way they respond to you.

III.   Memorize each model, practicing it in your mind, until you have it completely down. Only then proceed to the next chapter. When you're through, pat yourself on the back, as you have memorized and learned what many Ph.D. holding psychologists have not. This puts you in the top 20% of persuasion artists and preachers in general. You deserve that pat on the back—trust me!

CHAPTER 2

The Language of Persuasion is God (Part 2)

Some people seem to have the gift of gab and effortlessly persuade others to their way of thinking; others do not apparently have that gift. Do you think some people are just not cut out to be influential, charismatic, and gifted when it comes to winning over others? You'd be surprised how many people believe so. When you get finished reading this chapter you'll have learned many secrets the top persuaders do not want you to know. They do not want you to learn these secret lessons, because they'd prefer to keep the world blind to this knowledge, so that they themselves can reign over others with a magic that is envied by the top leaders and professionals of every major profession.

> *"The hope of democracy depends on the diffusion of knowledge."*
> —*Epithet which hangs above Pogue Library*

In this chapter we are going to be covering two models of communication. One model is the Milton Model, the other the Meta Model. One model is linguistically coded with the intent of generalizing information, while the other is coded in specifics. After we cover these models the last part of this chapter will cover language patterns you will instantly be able to memorize and adopt so that you never have to question your ability to communicate effectively—ever again! You'll be able to, without thinking, communicate so effectively, in fact, that you will have people dripping over every word you speak, wanting to be in your presence to, like a sponge, soak up the sweet nectar of your highly potent and supernaturally influential messages.

The Milton Model Revealed

Milton Hyland Erickson was an American psychiatrist, family therapist, and hypnotherapist. As a young child he nearly died from polio. During one of his two bouts with polio, while bed-ridden, he began to use his faculty of hearing, to decipher which of his family members were entering the house he lived in, just by the sound the door made when it opened and closed. His sensory acuity threshold was increased as a result, and even more so throughout his professional life and, even so, all the way up until he died in 1980.

Milton loved to tell stories. He loved to communicate in abstractions and generalities. For this reason he has been coined by some as the Father of Indirect Hypnosis. From him, has sprung many schools of hypnotherapy and even indirect communication models, used to influence and persuade others without them even knowing they are being influenced. Many disciplines have adopted his model of communication to be more effective communicators, including: sales professionals, negotiators, interrogators, politicians, and leaders of companies small and large.

Why Should You Learn the Milton Model?

Two men, Richard Bandler and John Grinder, founders of Neuro-Linguist Programming, visited Erickson, and carefully studied his linguistics, while he worked with psychotherapy clients; and they coded his linguistic patterns into what they branded The Milton Model. You see, Erickson was a top expert in his field, and Bandler and Grinder, modelers as they considered themselves to be, believed that if they could model his language patterns, they could in turn be just as effective at communicating in the abstract, as Erickson himself was able to do. They were right, and this is why learning The Milton Model is so important.

Learning The Milton Model will give you an edge when communicating with others.

When I green in sales, I was mentored by a man who introduced me to The Milton Model. The day before I met this man, I had sold myself on the idea that I wasn't cut out for sales. My mentor, stopped me from making this mistake, and arranged it so I could ride along with him while he made sales calls. Incidentally, he was the top sales professional working for the company. I was blessed to have had the opportunity to work alongside him.

We only worked two hours that first day, calling on three brand new prospects, and every customer bought what my mentor sold. I was astonished by how easy my mentor made it look.

Some days later, my mentor taught me the Milton Model, and how to apply it to my sales calls. I have used it to create wealth from the profession of selling; yet, more than that, I have adopted it to many other contexts—even preaching!

It is easier to roll eyes than it is to learn something new that will change your life in a positive way forever. For this reason, I encourage you to adopt this model, because it will help you communicate with other people at the unconscious unaware level; something I call the Other Mind. It will help you help them suspend their disbelief, and acquire the desired end result from every initiative you endeavor to accomplish and fulfill successfully.

What is the Theory behind the Milton Model?

The Milton Model is comprised of several linguistic speech patterns. Keep in mind, how you apply these patterns, will be different from how Erickson himself would have applied them, as the context is entirely different; yet, you will be communicating the brilliance that was purely Ericksonian.

The Milton Model language patterns are divided up into categories; namely: (a) mind reading, (b) lost performatives, (c) cause effect, (d) complex equivalence, (e) presuppositions, (f) universal qualifiers, (g) modal operators (e.g., necessity/possibility), (h) nominalizations, (i) unspecified verbs, (j) tag questions, (k) unspecified referential index, (l) comparative deletions, (m) pacing, (n) double binds, (o) extended quotes, (p) ambiguities (e.g., syntax, punctuation, phonetic, and scope), (q) conversational postulates, (r) selectional restriction violations, (s) utilization, and (t) embedded commands/questions.

I want you to think back to our last chapter. By now, I have to assume you have memorized the various persuasion models. What I want you to recall now is the central and peripheral path we discussed related to the Elaboration Likelihood Model. Recall, even deeper, how the central route was the weighing of the pros and cons; while, the peripheral route was accomplished by changing minds through the bypassing of the deliberation process. The bypassing of the deliberation process, i.e. the peripheral route, this is what the Milton Model is all about doing. We're essentially talking in such a way that the conscious thinking processes are bypassed, to let us communicate more indirectly through the Other Mind, i.e. unconscious state of mind.

Linguistically what this theory is all about is communicating through generalities, in which we become artfully vague; speaking in the abstract, while even deleting and distorting information as we communicate with others. People do this all the time. We're always generalizing, presupposing someone catches our meanings, and in the process we're deleting direct nouns; replacing them with indirect pronouns, and we're distorting messages as they get rehashed and retold over and over again and again. You might call it human nature. You might call it something else. In neuro-linguistic programming (NLP) we label this type of communication the "deep-structure". When we cover the Meta Model, we call that type of communication, as you might guess, the "surface-structure". Some people even call the Meta Model the inverse of the Milton Model. However you want to perceive it, is not wrong.

If I were to say, "The more you read it, the more things will happen," straightaway, given the context of what we've been discussing in this section, you perceive this sentence as ambiguous. Your mind may already be dissecting this sentence, by asking a series of questions:

- "Read what?"
- "What things will happen?"
- "Happen in what way?"
- "Does this only apply to me reading it?"
- "Can I assume this happens to everyone who reads it more?"
- "Is this person telling the truth?"
- "How does this person know?"

- "Why does reading cause things to happen?"
- "Are you talking to me?"
- "Who are you exactly talking to?"
- Are you talking to yourself?"

You might even conclude that this statement doesn't make any sense. Had you not been informed of the nature of the subject matter beforehand, you might assume it makes perfect sense, without even having questioned it otherwise. Chances are you would have assumed that I was in fact talking to you, and that I was implying the more you read this book specifically, the more you'd learn about persuasion, and the better your preaching would become as a result of studying this specific material.

Let's look at what the Bible tells us about words, and analyze critically the verses themselves:

(2 Timothy 2:14) Of these things put them in remembrance, charging them before the Lord that they strive not about words to no profit, but to the subverting of the hearers.

(2 Timothy 2:15) Study to shew thyself approved unto God, a workman that needeth not to be ashamed, rightly dividing the word of truth.

(2 Timothy 2:16) But shun profane and vain babblings: for they will increase unto more ungodliness.

We have already come to the understanding The Word and God are one and the same from chapter 1. Now in second Timothy, we see mention of worthless words, such as blasphemous and hollow words. Various lexicons have various interpretations of these verses; however, they all seem to imply that these verses are advocating that God wants us to speak words that profit Him, which are weakening to other choices followers might take. God wants us to study to show that we are endorsed unto Him; taking liberty to divide the word of truth, rightly.

God is our language. Interestingly this ability to communicate linguistically and as aptly as we are able, is one of the first differences that separated us from all other creatures. We need to be discerning of the language we use, using it in a way that lets us bring others to Christ Jesus. There is potency in words. Words are the deepest part of who you are, and when people think about you, they think about your words. The more you learn about language and how to divide it rightly; namely, indirectly or directly, the more effective communicatory you will become.

The statement I mentioned, just now, the vague one, causes your mind to assume a context, and create meaning from what's there. We do this automatically through conditioning, by bridging the gaps in communication to make sense of what someone is trying to relay meaningfully. It is the meaning we seek to understand, not so much the words themselves. Vague messages may speak to multiple people on multiple levels—all differently.

Remember though: God is The Word, and what people get, in terms of meaning, are the meanings God gives them through The Word. If you speak the same words to 100 people, all, one-on-one, absent one another, then different people will sense different meaning from what you say; even saying the same exact words. Now, put the same 100 people together in your church, and speak the exact same words, there will be a group meaning that emerges, where God speaks to the group, while also some will interpret the words on a personal level, and find personal meaning, meant just for their own ears.

If you take the word God, for example, it is more ambiguous in scope than if you, for example, take the name Jesus. You can identify with the characteristics, and your perceived personality of Jesus, based on, yet again, The Word, as written in the Bible, and find more specificity in terms of meaning. The word God, may be more ambiguous in terms of a specific definition you can interpret through the five senses. This is the same phenomenon, ironically, that we have with language, and persuasion psychology models. There is a side which is ambiguous, and a side that is very clearly specific, which we might define as disambiguation. Equivocal or unequivocal we have these same natures within our own psyche. There is the internal part of us: the self-talk in which we carry on a conversation with ourselves or with God. There is also an external part of us: the spoken words we speak, to others and, also to God.

When we are persuading ourselves we often times do so through self-talk, when we influence a friend, we might call that a pep-talk. Back to our persuasion models from the first chapter, once more, when you pep-talk someone, you can be sure that they will elaborate on your spoken words, through their own self-talk, which you won't be able to hear, but can be sure is being said. Meanings are processed through the mind or brain, therefore being an internal process; that is, requiring processing.

It is interesting to me how the more abstract and vague a message is, the longer the elaboration on that message, and thus the longer it takes someone to respond to that message. When you deliver a very specific message, most often the person receiving that message is quick to deliver back a response, without thinking about the message. It is more automatic. Keep this in mind, because the Milton Model is all about indirect communication, and taking people, in their minds, to places that require greater elaboration, and extreme mental processing. Just like a computer, when the conscious mind tries to process more information than it can handle, like the computer, the mind slows down, and a person's critical faculty to discern and sort out information consciously is suspended; allowing information, in the form of suggestions, to slip into the other mind. Like a seed planted in the ground, by the winds, on accident, the ideas planted in the mind, likewise germinate and grow until they become full-blown belief structures.

How is the Theory of the Milton Model Applied?

The Milton Model learned just like any other model. All that is required is that you learn some patterns, which are theoretical, and then begin applying them to your preaching, and all communication interactions which require you to be persuasive. The model is not difficult to learn. The patterns, again, make for some rather ambiguous conversation, on your part. Fascinatingly, you'll learn rather instantly that most people, when you use these patterns, spouting them off with good intent, and as though they are the most natural thing you could have said in that particular context, will not have a clue you are even being ambiguous. For this reason, these patterns are very covert; making it so that you can persuade people to your side of any argument, quickly and easily, without them even knowing you're intentionally using a persuasion tactic.

Now, let's learn the Milton Model, and take in some example patterns to really drive home the model, so you can instantly learn it and start using it.

The Milton Model

Mind Reading Pattern

I know what you're thinking, but, you'd be wrong, because the mind reading pattern is not to be confused with metaphysical or psychic activity. The mind read pattern is simply a natural extension of communication we use, without realizing it, all the time. In fact, I just used this pattern in the very first sentence of this paragraph. I made an assumption. The interesting thing is I can make an assumption about anything, and even if you were not thinking it, you are now. For this reason, this pattern is very powerful for reframing the direction of a conversation. It is powerfully used by some of the top communicators for the purpose of getting your audience to think about whatever it is you want them to think about. All that is required is for you to say, "You're thinking ____" or "I know you are thinking ____" or look very seriously at your audience and say something like, "You need to stop thinking ____, because ____." For you to practice this pattern only requires that you fill in the blank about whatever you want your audience to think about. It really is that simple. I know you are excited now! See I just used the pattern, again, to make another assumption, and to focus your attention on excitement. Who knows though, maybe you were excited already, right?

Lost Performative Pattern

A lost performative is a statement made with authority and conviction, yet without a performer, i.e. person to back up the argument. It's fun using this pattern. So let's look at an example: "It is fun using this pattern." You assumed it was me, as I'm the one writing the book you're reading, but did it have to be me who said this? Not really.

As I was doing research for this book, I visited many churches and listened to many preachers, preaching. At one church, I walked into the service a few minutes late, and so I quietly made my way to an empty seat. The church was packed, and people were intensively listening to this preacher delivering his message. The first words I heard him say were, "Learning new things is great." He repeated this lost performative three more times in a row, pausing five to ten seconds after each time he said it, as if to imply it was serious business and you better think about what I just said. From what I could gather everyone in that audience was emotionally sensitive to these words, his intonation, and his delivery of the message. What I quickly realized, being the modeler I am, was that the preacher was actually asserting this sentence out of context. Actually, there was no reason to say it. His message wasn't even about learning. It was about tithing. I cannot tell you how many people in the audience who said, "Amen, pastor! Preach it!" because I heard so many, I was floored in the affect that simply spouting off this lost performative had on his congregation. Throughout the rest of the sermon, he spouted off so many lost performatives, that I lost count. I will share that he said, "It's important. It's important. It's important," at least thirty times during that sermon. Incidentally, he never did clarify what exactly was important, or who said that it was important. It's important to pay attention.

Cause Effect Pattern & Presupposition Pattern

Every time I think of this pattern, I'm reminded of my third-grade teacher. She taught me about if/then statements, which are cause effect statements. A cause effect pattern is one which it is stated that something causes something else. Truthfully, it doesn't have to be reasonable, or even true, but the very nature of the cause effect pattern is one that assumes reasonableness from the subject. If you don't believe me, you will now, because I'm using a cause effect pattern right this very second. When you go back and analyze that statement, then you'll see what you wouldn't have, had I not taught this pattern to you. When you use this pattern, most people will never question the validity of the statement. How do I know? After you play around with using them, you'll know what I know.

Notice in the above paragraph, I'm making several presuppositions. A presupposition is a statement in which I assume you will do something, to experience something else. For example, "After you play around with using them, you'll know what I know." I am presupposing you are going to play around with them. I'm also making a compelling and persuasive argument for why you likely will, which is you'll know what I know. I am actually saying, that if you don't play around with them, you won't know what I know. This is loaded; that is, if you don't do what I assume you will do, then you'll lose out on something. People do not want to be kept in the dark, they want to know you're secrets. In order to learn, you have to do something I suggest. I just did it again!

Complex Equivalence Pattern

A complex equivalence pattern is one that says something is equal to something else, or equally reliant on something else. When you learn to use complex equivalence patterns it means you'll have mastered language eloquently. Okay, that barely makes any sense, yet I wrote it for a reason, because I'm saying that "When you learn to use complex equivalence patterns," it is equal in value to mastering language eloquently. Is that a true statement? I'll let you think about that one, and form your own opinion. So the pattern is essentially, "___ it means ___" or "___ it makes ___" or "___ meaning ___"

I was at another church, listening to a sermon, by a very qualified preacher, and he said at one point during the sermon, "I have started so I will finish." This is a complex equivalent. It is saying that starting something is equal to finishing it. I'm telling you these complex equivalence patterns happen all the time. Teaching you this, reminds me of when I was a kid, and I told my younger brother and sister, "Mom put me in charge, so you have to do what I say." I used them even when I was a small child. I'm sure you have too! ←Watch out; mind read pattern alert!

Universal Qualifier Pattern

Jesus never did no wrong. We always do. We can't help it, because we're human beings. Mortals. Everybody is capable of doing better than they do, but nobody is aware of this fact. It's going to take minute to figure this out.

Okay, the above paragraph is filled with universal qualifiers. Basically, what they are, are words like always, never, all, none and every that quantify with the assumption that whatever is said happens without the possibility of not. If I tell you, everybody believes in something, you may very well agree with me, thinking that this sounds reasonable enough, by default, to agree with me on. If I say to you good things always happen to the children of God, you may agree with me,

but is it really true? Not really. There are bad things that happen to everyone. ←
Another one, watch out! Do bad things really happen to everyone? I've not met
everyone, so I cannot say for sure. I'm betting you haven't either. Anyway, now
you know what a universal quantifier is, and how to use it.

How might you use one though? Any thoughts? What about: God is always
here for you to lean on. Or: God loves everybody!

There was a pastor, I recall from my research, saying, "All you need in your
life is faith in God. All you need is faith in Christ Jesus. Say it with me... All everyone needs is Jesus." This makes for a very direct use of the universal quantifiers:
all, and everyone.

In the Bible, there are many uses of these universal quantifiers. Linguistically,
they create importance, surety, and conviction that what the person is saying is
absolutely true; rather, even, unquestionable. All you need to do is use this pattern, and you will achieve everything that is possible. ← Oops...another sneakily
inserted universal quantifier.

I listened to a preacher say something rather interesting not so long back. He
explained how people have a tendency to judge others by their professions. For
instance, someone might be a janitor in a school making minimum wage; judged
as someone uneducated, broke, low class, etc. On the other hand, a lawyer may
be judged as someone well educated, competent, wealthy, a good catch to a lucky
mate. A lawyer generally makes more, we can assume. A janitor makes a low
wage. The preacher explained, and I found this bit rather intelligent, that pay is
determined on the problem you are willing to solve. A janitor solves a problem
that is less necessary and therefore warrants less pay. When someone needs a
lawyer to stay out of jail, the value of a lawyer takes on great importance and
great value; therefore, lawyers can command greater pay. It all depends on the
size of the problem. If you have a rotten tooth, that is immensely painful, paying
a dentist hundreds of dollars for thirty minutes of his time seems reasonable. Paying a janitor hundreds of dollars an hour to sweep a hallway, seems less important, and a much smaller problem offers much less pay. The preacher said he
doesn't judge the janitor, he judges the problem the janitor is willing to solve. He
doesn't judge the lawyer, only the problem he's willing to solve. If you solve a
small problem you'll be compensated with small pay. Relatedly, if you solve a

large problem you'll likewise be compensated with large pay. Pay is determined by the problem you are willing to solve.

So why do I bring this up so randomly? I bring it up, because, recall the story of Joseph, in the Bible, in chapter 41, regarding Pharaoh's dream? Well, when Pharaoh called Joseph before him, he uses one such universal quantifier, i.e. "none" and Joseph, if you recall, was able to solve a large problem; a problem none could solve. Let's look at the scripture, and see exactly what was said:

> *(Genesis 41:15) And Pharaoh said unto Joseph, I have dreamed a dream, and there is <u>none</u> that can interpret it: and I have heard say of thee, that thou canst understand a dream to interpret it.*

> *(Genesis 41:16) And Joseph answered Pharaoh, saying, It is not in me: God shall give Pharaoh an answer of peace.*

Pharaoh revealing to Joseph that "none" could interpret his dream indicates that, in my opinion, that Pharaoh perceived his problem of not having anyone to interpret his dream, as a bigger problem than it probably was. His use of the universal quantifier "none" indicates that he had probably made numerous inquiries to others about his dream. Having no luck getting it interpreted, he was probably rather desperate. When he heard that Joseph could, this news probably pinned back his ears, and filled him with a sense of hope.

I recount this for you for so that you will get a better understanding of how universal quantifiers create certain convictions within people. They can even blow an insignificant problem into a full blown predicament that affects a person on a much deeper psychological level.

Modal Operator Pattern (necessity/possibility)

To get the most out of this book you should learn all of these patterns, which would make you an expert. I could give you an easy way to remember this pattern, so you do not forget it. I'm telling you, right now, you must never forget this particular pattern. It can't happen, okay?

The above sentences are crammed full of modal operators. Modal operators are words like: could, should, would, can't, must, etc. Modal operators of necessity create urgency and belief. If I say, you must get here straightaway, the "must" indicates I'm very serious. If I say, I can't help you, you believe me more so than if I were to say, I shouldn't help you, because "shouldn't" indicates that there is a possibility that I may still be willing to help you. The word "can't" is more definite and concrete.

Nominalization Pattern

A nominalization is when an adjective, adverb, or verb has been turned into a noun. In some cases this means adding a derivational suffix onto the verb. In other cases no derivation is needed, and the verb can be used interchangeably as a verb or noun, depending on the context. I should point out now that the word nominalization, itself, is a nominalization. It has been derived from the verb nominalize.

I know with absolute certainty that you bought this book because you needed a change. The intensity you must commit to these learnings in order to be a master is less than you think. Everybody goes through it, like you. Failure is not an option at this point. Your reaction is your motivation, and what starts this journey. Just remember, preaching is persuasion.

The above paragraph is, as you might have guessed, full of nominalizations. I present you with so many, and in a rather ambiguous context, so you gain some familiarity and knowledge regarding how you can apply them in your preaching. ←Wow...another sentence with many nominalizations (e.g., context, familiarity, knowledge, preaching).

In proper English, it is advised that authors stay away from using so many nominalizations, because it creates ambiguity and indirectness. For the purposes of influence and persuasion, it is advised, however; rightly so, since people are left to form their own cognitions regarding the meaning. It is difficult to argue oneself, when one reasons what is what, and what "what" means.

Unspecified Verb & Noun Pattern

Don't get frustrated. Lots of people experience frustration. I'm here to help. These three sentences I've just relayed all contain unspecified verbs. An unspecified verb causes the reader, or in the case with your preaching, your subject, to mind read what you mean. An unspecified verb pattern is when you leave out details about the action, causing an unclear meaning. If, for example, I say, you're getting this easier than most, you might wonder, if you're particularly clued in, what is meant by "getting"? You might question, "Getting what specifically?" Also in this sentence I've given you an example of an unspecified noun, as well; namely, because I've deleted the noun. You would possibly like to question, "Most, meaning what? Most people? Most preachers? Most men? Most women?" The context is not clear. Most people will fill in the gaps with their own assumptions. ←Shucks…I've presented another unspecified noun, and verb, in this sentence. See how easy it is to do? ← Incidentally, do what? And, what is it? (Did it again!) ←And again.

Tag Question Pattern

So far these patterns are fairly easy, aren't they? You should assume the rest to likewise be just as easy, shouldn't you? Isn't is so, people are able to do more than they think they are capable of doing? You know what I'm doing, right, because I would wonder if you didn't.

Clearly the above paragraph, in fact every sentence, contains a tag question pattern. A tag question gets instant agreement from those you're preaching to. Not everyone knows this, but a tag question can come at the beginning of a sentence, the middle of a sentence, and most frequently, of course, at the end of a sentence. We basically tag them on, DON'T WE? Of course you want to agree with me, do you not? I thought so. ←Mind read pattern, right, you do remember, don't you? ←Two tag question patterns in one sentence? Yes indeed (e.g., *right*, and *don't you*). Incidentally, did you catch the deleted/unspecified noun that should come after 'remember'? Also, the unspecified verb 'do'! Lots of sneaky artfully vague language, isn't there? ←That's right. Just agree with me. It's easier, right? ←Good answer!

Unspecified Referential Index

We like things that are unspecified. The sentence I just stated, you might have mentally associated with the title: Unspecified Referential Index. The truth is, the sentence lacks a reference. Think of it like this. If I came up to you on the street, one stranger to another, and said, "We like things that are unspecified," besides thinking I'm a nut, what would you be thinking? You might question, for a moment, using self-talk, which I wouldn't be able to hear, since self-talk is something you do in your head, to mentally make sense of something, and then once you thought about it, would have come to some conclusion about what I meant, and why I might have said, what I said. You might have guessed that I was referring to a set of directions someone had given me, in which they weren't specific, and because of not being able to find where I was going, I was venting to a perfect stranger, trying to get moral support. I mean, really, we could play the guessing game all day long, but until you asked me to specify a reference regarding what I was talking about, you really wouldn't have a clue about what I meant. You might pretend to however. In fact you might convince yourself you actually knew. You really wouldn't though. ← Really wouldn't what, specifically?

Comparative Deletion Pattern

You have improved a lot without realizing it. It's better to be where you're at now. Now is where you're time is best spent. All the preceding sentences, as you've come to expect, I suspect, are comparative deletion patterns.

A comparative deletion pattern is where a comparison is made, but where what it's compared to is deleted.

Someone feeling inferior to another person may say, "She's better than I am." But better than what? The "what" is deleted, notice. Can you comprehend the ambiguity in such a statement? Most people, whom you'll be preaching to, will not. This is why ambiguity is so effective, when it comes to by passing someone's critical faculty, or what our psychological persuasion models would label bypassing deliberation processing. Why this is, has to do with the very word ambiguity, which is a close relative to doubt. Doubt denotes uncertainty, and ambiguity denotes confusion, and when someone is confused about something it is usually because they don't have all the facts. By creating persuasive arguments that are grounded in ambiguity, there is less chance someone will be critical, because they are in one sense too confused by the ambiguity to be form a clear judgment based on clarity. Most often your subject will fill in what has been deleted, or make assumptions about what has been generalized, or reform in what way they wish that which has been purposefully distorted through the tool of language. I really do know that you're better than you think, so you might want to quit thinking, as you're better off, aren't you, when you do. ←Quite a bit of ambiguity in this statement. Can you identify all the patterns present in this sentence? What about: mind read pattern, modal operator pattern, unspecified referential index pattern, tag question pattern, unspecified verb pattern?

Pacing Leading Pattern

You've taken in a lot up to this point. A lot has been given to you. You're still reading, which is positive. You'll start to, if you haven't already, to get some profound insights soon. These will likely be unexpected.

The above paragraph is a pace. Pacing is when you start by taking the subject through some observable experiences. This is done so the subject starts to mentally agree with you and inwardly and automatically says "yes". Then after pacing several unarguable statements, you lead with a plausible persuasive argument. In this example above, I paced sentence after sentence, and then finally stated: You'll start to, if you haven't already, to get some profound insights soon. In one sense this is a mind read pattern, also to make the lead statement more believable, I assert that bit about "if you haven't already" –and, this small add in adds credibility to the argument I am making, and propels me to the authority or expert which makes it all that more persuasive.

Double Bind Pattern

A double bind pattern is essentially the alternating choice close in sales; regarding the sales professional saying to the potential customer: "Do you want to use your pen or mine to sign the agreement?" Of course, not signing the contract is not an option. A double bind pattern takes pressure off of a heavy decision, makes it easier to make a decision by having only to consider an easier decision. Deciding which pen to use is easier than signing your life away on some contract.

In preaching, you can apply this pattern in a variety of ways. You might, for instance, say something like: Are you only paying your tithe today, or are you going to also help out our mission fund? It's up to you of course. This type of double bind doesn't suggest that they are not going to even pay their tithe. It assumes they are going to pay the tithe. Alternatively, you might phrase it: Do you want to donate a hundred dollars to the missions fund today, or just fifty. Less than fifty is not given as an option. Not donating is, again, not an option.

Extended Quote Pattern

An extended quote was taught to me by my friend Kevin, who said, "Extended quotes are a powerful way of deflecting attention off of you, and onto someone with more perceived authoritative value." Kevin of course was the authority, and since he wasn't there, people, like you, believe Kevin, whereas you might question that statement if I had said it outright.

So an extended quote is simply borrowing a name, and attributing something you want to relay to your subjects, as coming from that authority. Jesus said, "Behold the sower went out to sow..." Think of how many seeds have been sowed by the faithful, since Jesus said those words.

To create your own extended quote pattern, you can use the following template: My friend, (name), said, "___." Fill in the blank with whatever you want them to believe or focus on.

Again, we're being indirect in our communication, attributing something to someone else having said it; specifically, so that we take attention off of ourselves. If we say it, it might not be true. If someone else says it, chances are it is true. The person not there, certainly isn't trying to persuade us to do something. The person standing in front of us, however, very well could be. That's why this pattern is so useful to persuasion artists.

If you want to create even more confusion you can nest extended quotes inside other extended quotes. I was down in Houston, Texas, several months ago, and visiting the Wisdom Center, and I heard Dr. Mike Murdock say, "Your harvest is whatever you hold on to. When something leaves your hand, it gets multiplied. If it doesn't leave your hand it stays the same. My dad, said, 'Mike, you're the first person in the Murdock family, to ever give a $100 seed faith offering.' I only do, I said, what God tells me to do," he said to me.

Ambiguity Pattern

In the Milton Model there are four distinct ambiguity patterns recognized:

- ☐ Syntax: word order meaning.

    - ○ Example: We are understanding people. (Is this saying we are understanding? Or, is it saying: we understand people?

- ☐ Punctuational: Deleted punctuation which causes confusion.

    - ○ Example: I've been doing this a long time ago seems like yesterday.

- ☐ Phonetic: Homonyms (e.g., Your, You're)

    - ○ Example: A part of you in apart from me. (apart/a part)

- ☐ Scope: The scope of what is being conveyed could convey more than one meaning.

    - ○ Example: Confusing conversations can create confusion. (Conversations that are confusing? Or: Confusing conversations?)

Conversational Postualate Pattern

A conversational postulate pattern is phrased as a yes or no question; however, it is phrased as such through intonation to require a behavioral response. For example, "Are you able to turn to John chapter 3, verse 16? The question is asking for a yes or no answer; rightly so, most probable someone would open up their Bible and start flipping to that specific verse.

Why this is important regarding persuasion contexts is that it is a very indirect way of gaining compliance, because the person complying doesn't perceive you as telling them what to do; you're merely asking a question. Questions asking is a lot more passive and roundabout than telling someone to do something. Questions create choice, and the option to back out, but because its asked in this manner, people are likely not to back out and rather give in and comply—exactly what you want them to do!

The book you hold in your hand knows a lot more than you're reading into it knowing. This is an example of a selectional restriction violation pattern. A selectional restriction violation pattern is when you attribute human characteristics, such as emotions, to objects and beings which cannot by definition experience those conditions and states. For instance, a book cannot know things; it's not human and doesn't have a brain.

I like to refer to this pattern as the metaphor pattern, because people tend to think in terms of metaphors whenever someone uses this type of patter. I got rid of my cell phone, because it grew very tired of receiving phone calls all day long. This sentence is attributing the state of tiredness to a cell phone. Things that are not alive cannot become tired. As a result, the subject perceives the metaphor being that too many phone calls makes me tired and as a result is not preferred by me. Again, this is very indirectly conveying the message. If need be, this argument's assumption, by the subject, should the subject decide to challenge my statement, gives me leeway to argue. Had I been direct in my communication and said, "I got rid of my cell phone, because I received too many phone calls, which tires me out," the subject might have assumed that they were partially responsible for my irritation and frustration with cell phone ownership. Phrasing it metaphorically, using this selectional restriction violation pattern, takes away the tendency for someone to feel threatened, hurt, or blamed for why I no longer own a cell phone.

From the preaching context, a pastor might say something like, "The pews are sad, because there aren't enough people sitting in them today." Such a statement may infer metaphorically that the problem is too few people showing up for church. Had the same pastor come out and said directly, "More people need to start coming to church," it may have been somewhat off-putting and put undue pressure on those who did attend to never miss, even when warranted. By associating a feeling of sadness, it creates sadness in the subjects listening to the pastor's message.

Utilization Pattern

Just by reading this book, you're learning a lot more than many ever learn. Just by giving this your attention, you're escalating your abilities in a supernatural way. The preceding two sentences are using utilization.

Utilization is when you take something obvious that the person is doing and create an argument for causation implying what they are in actuality doing, is causing something else to happen as a result.

Another example would be, "Your eyes are open, and you're reading this sentence, and that is causing you to gain more knowledge." Is this statement really true? Maybe not! But, and really get this, it's quite plausible, and very possible and likely that had you not been aware of my suggestion you would have accepted it as fact and believed what I said to be true.

Utilization is simply taking a resource at your disposal and using it to accomplish something else. Because you now understand this you'll use it successfully to persuade people to do what you want them too. ← Another utilization pattern!

Embedded Command & Embedded Question Pattern

Get what I'm about to say, because if you do you'll become more insightful and more powerful in your persuasion preaching. Do you know you can get what I'm saying, and take your persuasion to another level? In the preceding two sentences I have imperative suggestions covertly embedded. In sentence one, there are two: get what I'm about to say, and become more insightful. In the question that follows it, are two: get what I'm saying, and take your persuasion to another level. These commands are embedded, and when spoken enunciated, as if to mark them out of the statement or question. We call this analogue marking when we mark out an embedded command or suggestion so that it become received at the unconscious level, i.e. through heuristic processing.

Very often when you'll be preaching you will apply, knowingly or not, these types of embedded commands, to influence your subjects to take certain unconscious actions. These types of embedded commands are also useful for priming a person to take an action when eventually a direct command, relevant or the same as the embedded command, is given.

An application I have noticed this happening a lot in preaching is when a pastor says, "Listen to me." An embedded command structure I've witnessed many pastors using is: "When you...Listen to me now...Take notice of what God has done for you already." By reiterating this command, repeating it over and over, it starts to take effect and the audience stays focused on the message, and become affected by the persuasive message—taking massive action as a result.

Adverb -LY Pattern

Rightly up to now you have learned the various patterns in the Bandler-Grinder Milton Model. This pattern, the adverb –ly pattern is an extra bonus for you. Adverbs which end in –ly take the attention of the subject and focuses it on the adverb ending in –ly; rather than focusing it directly on the message being spoken. For this reason, I include it in this chapter, because it seems to belong, for it functions the same.

Clearly, you know what I mean, don't you?

I'll just present you with a list of several I have heard the successful preachers using, as well as other powerful influencers.

- Quickly
- Clearly
- Obviously
- Regrettably
- Fortunately
- Happily
- Suddenly
- Patiently

To give you a greater sense of what I mean, when I say they detract from the message, just consider this example:

Happily, she got cancer and died.

During a workshop I told a young man exactly this, with a smile on my face expressing great joy and excitement (I wanted to be congruent with the word 'happily'), and the young man only heard the "happily" part of my sentence. Next I asked him, "What do you think about that?" His response was: "Wow! That's awesome!"

Then I asked someone else randomly from the audience who looked as if she had been paying attention without any external distractions, and her response was, "Yes. That woman is blessed, indeed."

Then I brought both of them up, to sit on stage, and repeated exactly what I had said, and very deliberately went slow enough so that they would get the meaning of the sentence. Both of them blushed and I reassured them that it wasn't them, as much as it was the brilliance of linguistics.

Many times on telethons where preachers are raising money for some charity, the organization, or to line their pockets, they will use the word "Quickly" when having those at home go to the phones. Next time, if you ever do watch one, listen to how many times the preacher says, "Quickly! Quickly, go to the phone. Quickly! Quickly. Delayed obedience is disobedience! Quickly. Quickly! Quickly go to the phone. Quickly. Right now. Quickly!" The preacher will likewise be reflecting in how fast he speaks these "quickly(s)" and possibly snapping his or her fingers or clapping or making some quick motion. Think about this for a moment. I mean, why is it so imperative that at right that very second someone in the middle of the night, the earliest hours of the morning, go to their phone and donate a thousand dollars to a televangelist ministry? Why can't the viewer take his or her time and make an informed decision about whether they want to part with their money or not? Obviously, you know the answer to this. ←Another –ly adverb, and a hidden mind read pattern. Be honest, did you catch the mind read pattern, or did it go under your critical faculty's radar? ← How can a 'critical faculy' possess something like a radar? Yes, that's right...a selectional restriction violation pattern. If it went under your radar, then you have now experienced this lesson, to know that these –ly adverbs truly are a powerful persuasion pattern.

What if You Apply the Milton Model to Your Preaching?

You can expect that if you apply the principles of ambiguity as outlined in the Milton Model you'll have a wider range of ability; regarding, how you communicate. You can look at the model as a linguistic tool-box that allows you a wider range of skill and ability.

Jesus spoke in parables in Matthew, Chapter 13. I will be covering his parables in the next chapter of this book; that is, when we get into storytelling, and how effective story telling can be applied to persuasive preaching. For now, just keep in mind, that ambiguous messages can be profoundly affective on your subject's psyche.

By now, you likely already have a good idea in some respects about how you might use this information I've shared with you pertaining to the Milton Model. My suggestion is that you meditate on this lesson, and let some ideas surface, so you extend your knowledge beyond merely a conceptual framework. In other words, do not get bogged down in the fine details; rather, determine what is useful for you and your preaching, considering who you are and what your values are, and then take what you need, and leave behind what does not apply to you specifically.

The Meta Model Revealed

The Meta Model, like the Milton Model, was created by Dr. Richard Bandler and Dr. John Grinder in 1975. When we think about the Meta Model, we have to go back in time and look at Alfred Korzybski's notion that "The map is not the territory." Essentially, what we mean when we say "The map is not the territory," we're actually talking about how the information that comes in through our senses; in which we process in our brains and make sense of, is not actually the reality that is out there. It is rather, our mental representation of the reality around us. So it's actually just an impression or a map of reality, but not actually reality. It is through that map that we navigate through life and formulate our own conclusions based our own experiences. This is important because everyone has their own unique experiences –and, no two people have exactly the same life experience.

What we can conclude is collectively people tend to have certain experiences that are similar. This is how we are able to formulate social judgments and values regarding what is right or wrong. Laws of the land, take for instance, are created based around what is socially acceptable or not collectively.

The meta model, beyond Korzybski, takes into account Transformational Grammar identified by Noam Chomsky as well as taking into account the modeling of several successful therapists; namely, Fitz Pearls, Milton H. Erickson, and family therapist Virginia Satir. What came about as a result were the linguistic patterns that could either create change in an individual's life, or put obstacles in the way for change happening. The Meta Model is useful for holding people accountable for their own use of inexplicit language; that is, deleted, distorted, and generalized language patterns. These can be used to help people reconstruct their own mental maps of reality to allow change to happen. Whereas the Milton Model is used implicitly; the Meta Model is used explicitly as one communicates with others. They both serve two distinctly unique purposes: heuristic and systematic communication applications.

So when we looked at the Milton Model, we looked at the way language models sometime delete, distort, and generalize information when people speak and communicate. Most often this is unintentional and unconscious when it happens. As a result of the deletions, distortions, and generalizations people tend to "fill in the gaps" to construct, based on their life experience and experience with language in general, what exactly is your meaning. This is very assumptive.

Some people believe that the Meta Model is the inverse reflection of the Milton Model. I mean, where the Milton Model seeks to generalize, distort, and delete information, the Meta Model tends to work in the opposite direction; rather, asking someone to be more specific and well define what was actually meant when a message was delivered. This is direct form of communication, which is void of ambiguity to the extent possible.

People often formulate beliefs constructed by life experiences, sensory perceptions, and a lifetime of respondent conditioning (formulating thought habits which have turned into beliefs over time). They come to certain conclusions based off of distorted, deleted, and generalized information. Take the context of selling for example: Sales professionals know all too well that if you can show the potential customer that "everyone" is buying your product; using testimonials, etc. that people are much more likely to jump on board and purchase it too. They do this because of the generalization that they make in their mind about your product—assuming everyone is purchasing it—when in fact, only some people (a tiny minority) have purchased it. When people formulate mental arguments in their minds the tendency is for them to lose an element of specificity, which could easily challenge their belief, opening up the belief to the possibility of collapsing altogether so a new belief might take affect instead—for example, believing you are depressed, when actually you're smiling all the time, happily natured. Many people become delusional by rhetoric and other persuasive messages being brought forth indirectly with ambiguity and confusion as the central techniques used to influence them. This false impression can lead to several problems formulating—barring the subject from transforming for the best, escaping delusions.

The Meta Model, chunks down, whereas the Milton Model chunks up. The Meta Model is distinctly specific in focusing attention. The Milton Model is distinctly abstract in focusing attention. In organizational behavior we find heads of organizations (e.g., directors/CEO's) tending to focus more abstractly; rather, contemplating the "big-picture" of all the moving parts. Those employees at the foundation level of an organization tend to think more aligned with specifics; rather, focusing on their specific function and how to accomplish it, irrespective of consideration of other departments and functions happening all around them. When communicating both models serve a usefulness. Up-to-now we have explored the usefulness of the Milton Model, now let us turn our attention over to the Meta Model.

Why Should You Learn the Meta Model? What is it?

You should learn the Meta Model, because there are going to be times when you are going to need to communicate on a level of specificity—challenging the statements of others in discussion. So let's put this into a context to give some contrast to why you need to know the Meta Model. Let's take for example, as a case in point, where you happen to give a sermon. Let's assume you're using ambiguities throughout your sermon, because you want to communicate on multiple levels and get through the clutter and noise your congregants have experienced from

past sermons and other religious messages they've taken in through various chan-
nels. Now, let's say you have someone after the sermon want to talk to you in
private counsel, because they were interested in what was conveyed through your
delivery and message, and would like to discover more from you.

In this type of situation, a better communication resource might be the Meta
Model. This model will allow you to communicate specifics with that individual.
Another application might be that someone is having some emotional conflict
and there's an incongruence in relationship with their beliefs and their emotional
capacity to intuit what they feel is right, versus what their critical mind is telling
them. As a result of this incongruence they want to get some counseling and advice on what they can do. So maybe what you're giving them is a persuasive message, which aligns with the overall intention behind the message pertaining to
what you want you want your audience to take action on and accept, and maybe
this individual is finding it challenging to accept the message. So now you're sitting face to face in your office, and during this confrontation they are speaking
generalizations, distorting information as they communicate, and deleting important particulars. Because of this, and because of your knowledge of the Meta
Model, you're able to use the Meta Model Violations to challenge what they say
against your message which is in conflict with their mental model of the world.
By using this model you can create some rapid change to happen for this individual, and allow these changes to take mental affect inside the mind of your arguer.

If you want a broader, more logical reason for why you might want to master
the Meta Model I can give you a reason: You may want to communicate more
effectively. When people are confused, or when they are unsure about the message you have presented to them in the abstract language of the Milton Model,
so for a more logical thinker, who is habituated towards applying critical thinking
to every argument put before them, you might want to mirror this by being critical of their persuasions and language that they are using to criticize your message. This can put you in greater rapport with the individual, make you the alpha
communicator, and lessen the chances they will mentally dispute you again. At
this point you're able to communicate on two levels with anyone you come
across. You're able to communicate using abstractions, while also able to talk specifics about anything you like as the need presents itself.

Meta Model Violations, by the way, can be viewed as challenge questions—for example, when someone approaches you with the comments, saying: "My faith is weak," you can respond by asking back, "How do you mean by weak specifically?" This challenges them to communicate more specifically and in the process opens them up to better understanding regarding what they're feeling emotionally, but which is hard for them to articulate into words. Opening up dialogue creates greater rapport and understanding and helps them influence and persuade themselves, while attributing it to you and your listening ear.

A better way, maybe to approach your reason for why you should learn this model, is, to simply state it in the obvious, so you can communicate persuasively using artfully vague language, affecting them emotionally, selling your message through the deep structure of communication, and creating a loyalty beyond reason from your subjects, while also being able to communicate back to them using surface structure communication that challenges them to speak directly and in a way that they must always be justifying to you their logic and reasoning. Faith, after all, doesn't require critical thinking; rather, it requires one to blindly follow the messenger, without question. Those who question your authority and who act critical should be directly dealt with critically, by forcing them to challenge their own language through Meta Model Violations being applied.

Let me turn your attention now to the Meta Model. We'll examine it to make sense of it, so you can begin instantly applying it to your interactions with others. The more you practice using Meta Model Violations with those you communicate with the more you'll appreciate these models of communication. The true value can't be expressed in words; rather, the true value comes in through application and scrutinizing the language of others. When you apply these models you'll see how they can work for you to make you more persuasive.

How is the Theory of the Meta Model Applied?

With the Milton Model information is taken in and interpreted on a deep level, creating an experience for an individual. What the Milton Model does is let people interpret information through their own experiences. The Meta Model makes explicit the search for elicitation of the deep structure of information.

In Latin, Meta is a word representing the concept of "being above" or "being about" so the Meta Model is a model which uses language to clarify language. Just like a camera has a filter that can alter information, human beings also have filters, which can distort information as well. These distortions are based on our experiences which are stored deep in our minds, which when surfaced the information gets filtered and expressed through language, the meaning of the experiences get altered representationally.

We can also, through scrutinizing, understand how various contexts are alterable, which can also change the experiences we have carried perceptually.

Distortions

The first set of Meta Model violations we observe in the Meta Model are distortions. Misrepresentations occur when we alter or distort the meaning of our experiences. Under the category labeled distortions are the subcategories: presuppositions, complex equivalence, cause effects, and mind reading. You'll notice these categories are found in the Milton Model. The difference here is that now we are going to observe how we can change experiences by correcting the semantic ill-formedness of an individual's language.

Presuppositions

So the first subgroup are presuppositions. I like to think of presuppositions as assumptions—for example, "You can't do this because of this." Or, "When you do this, you can assume that this is going to happen." Or, "After you do this, this will happen as a result." Take for a more specific example: "After you learn the Meta Model, you are going to be able to communicate with people in a way that encourages them to reassess and change their mental maps by changing their language.

We have to inquire of ourselves, "What else has to be true for this sentence to make sense." In other words, ask a question that will let the person making the statement become aware information they haven't yet considered in their conscious awareness. How we challenge these Meta Model violations specific to presuppositions would be to ask questions like, "Am I to assume ___?" Or, "Are you presupposing that ____, will occur?" Or, "Are you saying that ___ is happening? Or, "Are you assuming that this is going to happen?"

In Socratic Dialogue, which we'll cover in a later chapter, Socrates was able to challenge a person's language, much in the same way we're able to challenge language using the Meta Model, especially with regard to generalized presupposition statements; that is to say, Socrates might say something like: "Just so I can be sure I am understanding you correctly, you're essentially saying ___?" Then as a follow-up to them saying "Yes. That is exactly what I'm saying," we then might ask a how questions—for example, "How do you know that? Or, "How do you know this is true, just so I can be sure I am understanding you correctly."

Complex Equivalence

Back when we studied the Milton Model, we learned that something is equal to something else. These complex equivalence patterns are, for example, when someone says, "I'm going to the store, meaning I'm going to buy groceries." Now this seems logical; rather, for the fact people do go to the store generally to buy groceries; however, people go to the store for other reasons as well. So we cannot say that going to the store is equal to everyone in the free world buying groceries. It simply is not a true statement.

So how we challenge a complex equivalent is simply to ask how questions—for example, "How does this equal this?" Or, "How does this mean this?" Or, "How does going to the store mean you are going to buy groceries?" You may find some answers that are quite common sense. In many cases you'll find answers that don't make a lot of sense, which can have a challenging effect on a person, challenging their logic and reason.

By challenging someone, forcing them to prove that something equals something else, and vice a versa, you can actually help the individual to reconnect with their sensory experience; in other words, the experience that happens based on the information coming in through their senses, with conscious awareness.

Cause Effect

Often times when someone elicits a cause effect statement they are actually giving away their personal power, i.e. "I cannot do this, because of this!" Or, "This person made me do this." Recall the earlier psychological persuasion models, specifically the Attribution Model. In cases like these, individuals are attributing an external factor to why they are not able to be successful doing something.

Many times when someone makes a cause effect statement you'll get insight into how this person's beliefs govern their experiences, and how beliefs affect circumstances. So to challenge such a violation, you might ask, "How exactly is this true?" Or, "How did you come to formulate that opinion?" See, they're taking this to be a fact, and now we're delimiting it from the view being an opinion.

If someone says, "Well, she made me rob the bank!" You might ask, "Well what else can she make you do?" And this is going to get them to reevaluate whether or not she made you do something or if some other cause happened to produce that particular effect, i.e. robbing a bank. In this particular type of questioning you're giving back control to the individual to they can assume responsibility for themselves, and not hold other people in control over them. So you have to be careful about how you challenge these Meta Model violations.

Mind Reading

Mind reading happens all the time. This is when we assume something someone else is thinking without any evidence for it. When it comes to faith, and convictions attributed to God, very often we see people make statements; namely, claiming to know something they do not know, or pretending to know something that they don't know. Faith is belief without evidence, and ironically enough, faith and mind reading share common ground.

Often when you talk to someone, and you're observing their body language, you might assume, for instance, that their body language is saying one thing, while it's saying something entirely different. People, experiencing this, may make a statement, claiming: "Well, you're not really following me here, are you? I know for a fact you're not!" if the person is looking confused.

Another very common mind read pattern is when someone says, "I know what you mean," or "I know how you feel," or "I'm with you there, so I can absolutely relate with what you're saying."

In Sales someone might tell one of their cohorts, "Oh yeah! This customer is ready to buy! I know it!" Realistically, they don't know for sure, because unless you're in someone else's mind, and you happen to be them, you cannot be completely sure 100%. You might suspect, or have in your mind a mental probability, but suspicion alone doesn't mean you're right!

If you want to challenge someone who is mind reading you can ask a question like: "How do you know that?" or "What evidence supports that theory?" or "What exactly was seen or heard by that person to make them think that?" or "How do you know what I was thinking? or "How do you know ___?"

A step by step process in terms of how they derive their conclusion, which we know, of course, is a false conclusion, or a conclusion not founded on any kind of grounded basis. Then we can simply ask as a clarification, "So is that your only evidence?" Then get them to clarify even more specifically until which time they clarify themselves out of the knowing, which possibly will reveal they don't know or that they even possibly doubt what they claimed to know.

Generalizations

Generalizations involve generalizing information, which fall into four different categories; namely: (a) Universal Quantifiers, (b) Modal Operators of Possibility, (c) Modal Operators of Necessity, and (d) Lost Performatives.

Universal Quantifiers

When we looked at the Milton Model I taught you that these universal quantifiers are statements made using words like: all, every, never, nothing, everything, and always. Types of statements made using these universal quantifiers make the generalization that "every" instance of a claim something happens. In reality, we know that the possibility that "every" time an even occurs the same result will remain, is impossible—given the fact that we have not experienced "every" happening and thus cannot know for sure. Again, this goes back to claiming to know something we do not know with absolute certainty. When someone uses a universal quantifier in a statement, you can often times get a general idea the individual is rigid and inflexible when it comes to this aspect of their world model.

When correcting these violations often we flip the argument on its reverse side and ask questions that are a counter example to the statement they have told us—for example, "We always go to church on Sunday!" A counter example would be—"Always go to church on Sunday?" or "So you've never missed a single Sunday, ever?" When you ask a question like this, it causes the subject to revisit their memory, re-experiencing their life history, and re-evaluate the statement they made to determine if it is actually a statement which is true or false. You might ask, as a clarifying question: "Even when you were your sickest, you went to church on Sunday?" or "Even when you were on vacation you attended church on Sunday—so you've never ever, whatsoever, missed a single Sunday church service anytime throughout your life?" Certainly, as you ask these questions, you're putting emphasis on the words which are the universal quantifiers used by the individual who has just made the statement.

Modal Operators of Possibility

When we think of possibility we think of what's possible. As a linguist and a modeler, I use modal operators to describe certain parts of speech and language. Modal operators of possibility are limitations on a person's model of the world, and they actually highlight those certain beliefs. So when we look at modal operators of possibility, we're looking at words, as stated before when the Milton Model was discussed, words like: can, can't, choose, might, mightn't, possible, impossible.

Certainly problems do not always exist every instance you find someone using a modal operator of possibility—such as, "I can do this." Or, "I can do that." No, usually when someone uses only the negative forms of modal operators of possibility do we see problems begin to red-flag, and come to the surface of communication—for instance, "I can't do this," is a clear example of someone sharing a problem with us.

As the Gestalt therapist, Fritz Pearls, would say, "Don't say can't say I won't." This frees up the individual from their old limiting beliefs. So you can challenge modal operators of possibility through asking a variety of questions—for example, "What would happen if you did?" Or, "What would happen if you could?" When someone says, "Well I can't do this!" You could also ask, "What is stopping you from being able to do that?" Then you will be able to determine the problem behind, or the perceived problem behind that individual's perceived problem, so a solution can be determined.

Someone says, "Well I can't do something," you come back with, "Well how do you stop yourself?" This could be another question you could ask. Or you could even suppose what they are claiming not to be able to do is possible. You simply ask, "What would be the result if it were possible?" You could also say, "Suppose you do this, then what would be the result?" Now they are seeing past the problem and focusing on the possibility it could be true. Now they can mentally recognize the benefit of solving the problem.

Modal Operators of Necessity

Looking at modal operators of necessity we instantly find that we're looking at a person's model of the world, and their greatest perceived ideas regarding what is needed in their life. These types of words, being used by the individual are words such as: must, mustn't, have to, need to, needn't, should, shouldn't, ought to, and oughtn't.

When you hear someone speaking these words, these are red flags that the person is leaning on a notion they have a great need. A sales professional loves when they hear these types of words, because when someone says, "Well I should do it, but..." When these words are present in their language these are indicators that in their mind it is necessary for them to take a course of action or not. Statements like these limit belief constructs. Now what we're doing by correcting these violations are to ask questions pertaining to consequences or outcomes. When we do this we ask questions like, "What would happen if you did?" Or, "What happens when you don't?"

The individual then, may think about the reverse of their supposed outcome and consider the consequences (e.g., pros and cons) were they not to do what they thought they should. To clarify this point, assume someone says, "I really need to read this book." If you ask the subject, "What would happen if you didn't read it?" The response given back would relay a different perspective. They begin to consider things they haven't yet considered, regarding taking a different course of action. This point, though seemingly obvious to you, possibly, should not be taken lightly. I would underscore this idea of considering the inverse of doing what you think you should or must do. Even for yourself, you may want to really stop and pause for a moment and think about what would happen if you didn't do what you think you must. Often the answer will be liberating; especially, if you don't want to do what you think you must.

If someone says, "I have got to do this!" Or, "I ought to go there!" Or, "I should be there!" Or, "I must not do that!" Or, I have to go over there" I have to... I must not... I should be... I ought to... Or, place these onto to others—like for instance, "He has got to do something!" These are all modal operators of necessity. The thought that comes instantly into my mind when I think of them, which helps me remember them, and how they can be used is the idea of the blame game. The blame game is when you say, and we may all do this, things like: "She has to be stopped, because she's out of control." Or, "He has to stop smoking, as it is unhealthy." When people in your life judge you—playing the blame game—you just need to ask them to think about the consequences of not doing what they think you ought to. Ask questions like, "What will happen if she is not stopped?" Or, "What will happen if he keeps smoking?" These answers seem obvious, but when they are heard, it has a freeing quality. When the person receiving the judgment hears the answer to these questions they somehow recognize on a more important level, achieving a greater persuasion, to the reasons why it is in their best interest. People with habits may not want to be told what to do, but when they hear the likeliness of what will happen if they continue a bad habit, it is actually more convincing and persuasive and can lead to real change.

Lost Performatives

Lost Performatives are statements unsupported. These statements have lost an actor or performer. The actor or performer would be someone specifically who is performing a particular action. Typically, these are generalized statements—for example, "It's said, *Preaching is Persuasion* is the best book on influence and persuasion." The actor would be the person who says this, but notice, we do not know who this person is.

We see, many times, on the back of books, examples of lost performatives. These are statements like, "Intriguing and Inspiring!" Or, "Powerfully Original!" We take these opinions into consideration all the time when making a purchasing decision, but we rarely question the fact nobody actually is mentioned as making these claims.

When a person makes such a statement you can ask them questions which will put the actor back into the statement. For instance, asking, "Says who?" or According to who?" would bring back in the actor from the person making the statement so we could judge their authority over the claim. Sometimes people say, "People are able to do more than they think they can." Asking, "Who are these people, exactly?" forces the person making the statement to give a more specific answer, or else lose credibility. I've noticed when I've challenged violation that often people will give a reply that is also general. They might say something in response, such as: "Well, all sorts of people!" or "It is general knowledge that lots of people say these things!" They are saying these things to justify their statement, but continuing to challenge them with more clarifying questions can cause them to admit they don't know, but be careful, as some people will get annoyed or decide having a conversation with you is not worth their time. This approach may break rapport with the person you're engaged in conversation with, so you have to be careful and know the person well enough to know where the boundaries of communication begin and end.

Here's an example story I'll share with you about lost performatives. I was once selling high-end personal development programs for a company. When I called on a potential customer, using a Socratic Method sales approach, the person on the other end of the phone would say something like, "Failure is a given!" To challenge this violation, you might ask, "Who's destined for failure, and they might say, "I am." Then I might ask them, "According to who?" Then the person would either have to own that statement as their own, or else present another actor (e.g., someone else making that judgment who I could discredit, making it a mute objection). When people listen to their own statements it can be very painful in such an example, I would find. It may be the jolt of facing the symptoms of the problem that they need to help them change their opinions or to trust someone to help them make a change. This is around when I usually closed the sale. Ownership often is deflected, and not owned. When someone owns their own statements and come off of being dissociated from their problems, they begin to experience emotions that can affect them into change one they associate with those problems and symptoms.

Keywords to look out for when speaking with people are lost performatives like: People say ___, It is ___, It's ___, Many people ___, etc.

Who's opinion is that? Who say's so? Say's who? Who said that? For whom? Whom are you referring? These phrases can be used to challenge lost performative violations.

Deletions

Deletions limit a subject's model of the world. They do this by leaving out important information. Types of deletions include: (a) nominalizations, (b) unspecified verbs, (c) simple deletions, (d) comparative deletions, and (e) lack of referential index.

Nominalizations

When we discussed the Milton Model, we found that a nominalization is a verb, adverb, or adjective and turn it into a noun. Doing so we ask the question: "Would this noun actually fit into a wheelbarrow;" that is, is it a tangible noun or an intangible noun. An intangible noun could be a concept, idea, or some other defined notion that's concretely stated as a noun. The words: concept, idea and notion, are all, incidentally, nominalizations. You cannot take an idea, for instance, and put it into a wheelbarrow and take it somewhere. Many words that end in –ing are found to be nominalizations. Someone might say, "I have a knowing that God exists." "Knowing" in this case is a frozen process, which was nominalized from the action verb "to know".

Another way to think of nominalizations, beyond our wheelbarrow analogy, is to ask if you can smell it, taste it, touch it, hear it, or see it; in other words, use your senses to interpret it as an object. If not, you know you have a nominalization.

What I told you to keep in mind earlier, regarding a nominalization being a noun; something concrete taken from something fluid and moving—such as an action verb—for example, "to inform" verb becomes nominalized into the noun "information" what you do is simply take the nominalization of the sentence and convert it back into a verb.

So if someone says something like, "I don't understand this!" You can ask the question: "What are you not understanding specifically?" If the person answers, "My understanding is not clear," you might ask, in that case, "What is it you do not understand yet?" This frees the person to come off the distortion.

Unspecified Verbs

Unspecified verbs are missing content relevant to particular contexts. These verbs lack an actor or other content related information. A person might say, for example, "Traveling is so much fun!" What's missing is, "Where?" Maybe not all travel is always fun. Always, of course, would be construed as a universal quantifier; that aside, in this particular context, one might ask, "Traveling where specifically?" Or, "Traveling where is so much fun specifically?" The answer given in response might be, "Traveling to the Bahamas is so much fun."

Simple Deletions

Simple deletions are natural occurrences in communication. It is when a person, process, or thing, is simply deleted from a sentence—creating a sense of vagueness around the conversation.

To correct these violations, you're simply looking out for the missing link, i.e. missing information that would make the communication more meaningful. By becoming very specific, creating more detail, this is possible.

The metaphor I like, which helps me to recall simple deletions is: An artist who draws. You can draw a simple outline of an individual and it can still be enough information, to visually interpret that it is an individual. As the artist continues to draw the figure, more details are added, enriching the image. You can add so much detail the drawing becomes a life like representation of an actual person. The more detail something has, the more clearer it becomes, and the clearer the vision and experience becomes. What you're doing by gaining more information based on the type of questions you ask, you're actually like an artist, filling in the details, to create greater clarity around the message. By clearing up the distortion of the image the image takes on new meaning; meaning that the individual is revolving around whatever is being discussed can actually alter and change. It's as easy as that.

Let's take the example a statement made by someone saying, "I went to town yesterday." The words tell us the person speaking went to town, and did so yesterday. It doesn't tell us, however, where they went to town, or when precisely they went to town, it doesn't tell us the town they went to, or even the purpose they went to town. So the types of questions we might want to ask would include: "Where specifically did you go at in town?" The answer given would help provide more insight making the conversation more meaningful.

Comparative Deletions

A comparative deletion is when a comparison is being made—perhaps something is better than something else, or this is the best out of the bunch—these types of comparisons and those certain words like: good, better, and best. More or less, these give away the point the person speaking is giving away a comparative deletion.

Advertisers on television, using the medium of commercials, use comparative deletions all the time. Some advertising firms have gotten into trouble using such comparatives, because when you're making a comparison, stating emphatically that one product is better than another product, without proof, you may be making a false advertising claim. If you do not substantiate what you mean, providing a level of transparency in your claim, you may get a phone call from the Federal Communications Commission (FCC) or Federal Trade Commission (FTC).

There was a case not so long ago, as of the publication of this book, where a late night infomercial personality was sentenced to 10 years in federal prison, for misrepresenting a book he wrote, using similar terminology. You have to be careful how you represent information to the public. Making false claims that could injure people is not only unethical, it could be criminal.

A word like "better" to compare your product with that of another, without supporting facts can land a suit against your business. Best, well, that's a matter of opinion, because it's not making a direct comparison. When a company uses the word better, they better have proof to back up their claim that whatever they are claiming is better, is, in fact, better.

Because these are comparisons, we can ask question to correct these violations, such as, for instance, when someone says, "This is the best pizza in town." You could say, "Best compared to what other pizza?" It is possible, even likely, that someone making this claim, hasn't tried all the pizzas in a particular town. It's a matter of opinion.

When you hear someone say that something is better than something else you can challenge the comparison, i.e. comparative deletions, with a questions like, "Better in what way specifically?

Lack of Referential Index

Again, we mentioned lack of referential index, when we talked about the Milton Model. Now, we'll look at the violations that referential index causes when there are a lack thereof.

To restate what a lack of referential index is, it's: when there's a reference made to a person or thing, but which is unspecified, it's a lack of referential index. These can be statements that are experienced as more or less a generalization, but the deeper structure of the violation is the lack of reference for the representation. For example, you could say something like, "People are ugly." This is definitely a generalization. You can challenge the violation by asking, "Which people are ugly?" Or, "Ugly compared to who?" Or, "How do you mean by ugly? Or, more likely, you would ask, "When you say, "people," to whom are you referring to exactly?" A statement like this is likely to produce other violation by the answer. For example, if someone says, "All people." Well, we know straightaway that "all" is a universal quantifier. We could then challenge this violation, by asking, "You've met all the people in the world, to be able to make such a claim?" Certainly, the have not, so the answer they give should correct the violation. Also, the adjective "ugly" still has not been defined. It is still vague, and therefore still need an elaboration to gain greater clarity by what is meant.

We have now covered the NLP Meta Model and Violations. I've stated this Meta Model in the format I have, to make it easier to recall the various parts of the model. Practicing this model, and using it as a tool to become critical of other people's language, will help be able to communicate more effectively. Later when we cover the Socratic Method, you'll discover how these types of questions actually apply to this new model of communication. For now, let's learn one thing at a time, and learn it well, and then continue on learning more. As you finish this book, you should have a thorough proficiency with all the models and lessons taught in this book.

What if You Apply the Meta Model to Your Preaching?

By now, if you can't tell, we're being critical of what people are saying so as to not take for granted what they are saying. This is especially useful when someone is stating how we should agree with them; without providing any substance to support "why" we should agree. In essence we are forcing them to likewise question their own assumptions and persuasion arguments. Doing this creates changes in thought, emotion, reaction, and behavior—allowing for more rational and logical persuasions to surface. Keep in mind, when people persuade themselves, it is much more powerful and longer lasting, than when we tell them something persuasive and they believe it at face value without any logic or reason to support what we claim. This goes back to the systematic model of persuasion—the first model we covered in Chapter 1. If you refer back to the Milton Model, this would be more geared towards the quick changes, but which are less likely to be long lasting, which link back to the heuristic model of persuasion—a model more focused on emotional appeal and less on rational arguments. Both models have their place in persuasion, and both can be used to create the changes in behavior you want others to elicit.

Persuasion Patterns Revealed

Maybe this will be your favorite part of this entire book—many people might agree this section gives them instant skills in covert persuasion. When you learn each one of these patterns, ask yourself, "Do I notice my skills increasing more than I ever expected?" After you consider what I'm about to reveal to you, you'll start to take persuasion; that is, the Milton Model, Meta Model, all the persuasion models, and the Socratic Method Model (forthcoming), and linguistics and communication in general much more seriously—noticing everything everyone says to you all the time in all your interactions.

Why Learn Persuasion Patterns?

Persuasion patterns are easy persuasion language templates that will help you influence others without having to think about what to say next. They are easy to remember. They are language patterns that have proven themselves, and is why so many preachers in the "know" use them every single time they preach, and I will hesitate a guess and assume in all their communications with others.

I wish I had enough time and space to give them all to you here. Unfortunately it would fill up too many pages and take away from other platinum persuasion content that I have planned to give you in this book. Fortunately, I have it in the works, to put together a flashcard deck, because I think it will be really the easiest most practical way to help you learn them so you have them automatically. Since I'm writing this book now, I obviously do not have the flashcards created yet, so you'll want to keep checking back from time to time on our website: www.indirectknowledge.com so you can get them when they first come out. It happens often that these tools will sell out rather fast, so the quicker you get to the punch clock the better chance you'll have of being able to purchase them. Until you can get them though, practice religiously these patterns of persuasion I am feeding you now, because they will revolutionize your preaching and ability to persuade anyone to your way of thinking. It is amazing how many people email me after learning these patterns and using them—telling me how astonished they are by the results!

What You Need to Know About Persuasion Patterns?

Okay! Let me say this: there are two things you need to realize, before you learn these patterns:

I.   These persuasion patterns are going to take you to a higher level of persuasion. INSTANTLY

II. These patterns, without knowing learning everything else I'm giving you, alone, will not take you to the highest level you're capable of.

The fact that you're reading this book right now tells yourself that you already fall into a certain category. This book most certainly isn't for everybody. I make no denial about this fact.

Here's the deal. Starting this very moment I want you to suspend your disbelief regarding who you're capable of becoming. Really suspend it NOW, because from this moment on through the rest of the book you are empowered, excited, confident, possess absolute clarity, and 100% certainty that you have what it takes to be David after he killed Goliath. Imagine that feeling David must have possessed. Think about that, because after accomplishing something that unbelievable I have to fathom that David must have thought that he was capable of doing anything—you're capable of doing anything, right now! This is the mindset you'll have while learning all the rest this book has to teach you, and even long after you've read the book. Everything you do matters! Get that! Really get it!

Got it? Terrific! Now let's learn what the patterns actually are, and then we'll turn our focus over to how to implement them successfully—so they get you the outcomes you most desire. We're going to cover ten of them in the book, and you can certainly learn many more when the flashcards are made available on indirectknowledge.com. Here we go.

I.   Here's the deal. _____

II. Imagine this. Here you are _____

III. The fact that you're _____, means _____

IV. When you _____ do you notice _____

V. And let me say this. The true beauty of _____ is _____

VI. I have a feeling _____

VII. Get a hold of this. _____

VIII. I (you) cannot _____, until I (you) _____

IX. The more _____, the more _____

X. When you _____, then you _____

How Are These Preaching Persuasion Patterns Applied?

Everyone has certain linguistic patterns they lean on and use more frequently and out of habit than other patterns. We all do this.

Many students in middle school and high school copy and use certain phrases that have meaning to that group. The Valley Girl, "Like, really!" is one such example. In churches we call each other "brother" and "sister" so and so. These are more used out of respect. Different professions have their key industry verbiage. In fast food, for example, when carrying a pan or really anything throughout the back of the restaurant, the term "hot" is used. In sales, terminology like prospecting, and closing are common. In Church, "amen" or "preach it" are commonly said. These are said almost habitually—if not habitually.

Patterns arise when speaking one on one with individuals. Mostly, we're unconscious of these words and don't think about them. Others are usually unaware of the words we speak to them; that is, out of habit.

People learn on four levels of competence. In psychology this model is termed The Conscious Competence Learning Model. Namely, the four competence levels are: (a) unconscious incompetence, (b) conscious incompetence, (c) conscious competence, and (d) unconscious competence. Let's explore what is meant by these labels:

I.   Unconscious incompetence is when someone is not aware they do not know something.

II.   Conscious incompetence is when someone become aware of the fact they don't know something that could prove valuable for them.

III. Conscious competence is when someone has learned something consciously, but where conscious effort is needed (i.e., concentration) in order to recall it and use it.

IV.   Unconscious competence is acquired through repetitive practice until someone knows something so well that they do not have to consciously think about performing the task. In this case it becomes an unconscious task (e.g., driving a car without thinking about it).

Here's the deal. When you first begin practicing these language patterns, then you'll start to realize you do not know them whatsoever. This is because you're now aware of these language patterns—whereas before reading about them before now you weren't aware of them—thus you were *unconsciously incompetent* of them then. Now that you have been introduced to them you are experiencing *conscious incompetence.*

Imagine this. Here you are now, soon to start practicing them, using them as intentionally and often as you can, until you have them at the very least memorized. You cannot yet know them unconsciously, until you first know them at this stage of *conscious competence.*

I have a feeling that after you practice them over and over and over again you will be speaking them unconsciously, rather soon; meaning, you'll have arrived at the final stage of this learning model, i.e., *unconscious competence.* The more you practice, the more you'll have them down. The fact that you're reading this book, means you want to gain this unconscious mastery over these persuasion patterns to be able to instantly persuade anyone, anytime you like. Get a hold of this, because once you do, you'll be speaking persuasively without even knowing you are. And let me say this: the true beauty of speaking with persuasive eloquence is your covert power over others and how you affect them through your persuasions.

First you have to face where you're at now though. When you start anything new, do you notice how you take your learning for granted? I know I do. Not to worry though, because you'll have these ten patterns down, and be using them unconsciously and consciously as you desire to, before long at all.

The above paragraphs, which explain the conscious competence learning model have consciously adapted to cover all ten of the persuasion patterns. If you did not catch on to this fact, I encourage you to go back to the ten mentioned persuasion patterns, and then re ready the last four paragraphs before this one. You'll find that the patterns are embedded into the paragraphs, and to an unaware reader, they never would have noticed, would they?

Now let's take each of the ten language patterns and explore them in depth. I'll present each pattern, then an example, and then a purport for each one. Here we go.

Persuasion Pattern 1:

I.   Here's the deal. _____

- Example: Here's the deal. Learning these patterns, right now, will give you an edge like no other.

- Purport: This persuasion immediately elicits a proposition –and, likely one that is a good deal. People want a deal. This pattern also is a nice pattern for sharing attributes, advantages, or benefits of a message or point you want your congregation really getting. It encourages them to pay attention, and even can refocus attention that's been lost by your listeners.

Persuasion Pattern 2:

II.   Imagine this. Here you are _____

- Example: Imagine this. Here you are tithing out of every paycheck you receive, and you begin to start noticing how God is bestowing blessing after blessing on you.

- Purport: The "imagine this" part of the pattern is an awareness focuser. When people imagine something in their minds we want them to imagine that it is as real to them, as it might be, were it actually right in front of them. The other mind doesn't distinguish between what's real or what's has been imagined. Using an awareness predicate like "imagine" forces someone to think about whatever you want them to be thinking about. People cannot help it. If I were, for instance, to ask you to imagine a pink elephant, guess what...you just imagined a pink elephant. I persuaded you to think about something and you had no choice except to think about it. I'm right, right? The "here you are" part is leading them toward what it is you want them to think about. It could also be used to have them think about being in someone else's shoes (e.g., Here you are, David, and facing this enormous Goliath, and what do you do?)

Persuasion Pattern 3:

III.   The fact that you're _____, means _____

- Example: The fact that you're studying these persuasion patterns, means you will always have the upper hand in any persuasion context.

- Purport: The first half of this language pattern is where you'll list an obvious outward fact that cannot be argued. It could also be an internal or intangible fact from perhaps something the subject has told you about themselves or situation. The next part uses the complex equivalent "means" to equate that fact to a persuasive insinuation or suggestion. It could also be linked to an emotional benefit. Keep in mind the argument only has to be relatively plausible for your subject to accept it instantly as true (e.g., The fact that you're here means you really care.)

Persuasion Pattern 4:

IV. When you _____, do you notice _____

- Example: When you obey God, do you notice how God provides for you the perfect relationship, the money you need to do what you need to do, and the ability to do things you never knew you could do?

- Purport: In once sense this is a cause effect language pattern. I really like this language pattern for preachers, because it also creates this future pace; in other words, it takes people in their minds either back in time, or forward in time to consider whatever comes after the "notice" part. The other thing this pattern does is presuppose that whenever you do one thing, something else happens automatically whether you're aware of it or not. Even if the person is not aware and haven't noticed, they have now, at least in their mind. This is a very powerful language pattern that communicates with someone on multiple levels of persuasion. It even acts as a "Yes-Set" because the answer most almost always given is "yes;" confirming they agree with what you have persuaded them to agree to.

Persuasion Pattern 5:

V.   And let me say this. The true beauty of _____, is _____

- Example: And let me say this. The true beauty of God's plan, is the unfoldment of the truth in your life that is carrying you closer and closer to the brilliant life God has planned for you.

- Purport: The first part "And let me say this," serves as an indirect opener, that is permissive, and which lowers the resistance filter inside your subject's mind. The second part of this pattern paints a picture of beauty and wonder without the disbelief happening. The reason the incredulity is not present is because we've prefaced with the "Let me just say" part. Finally, the "is _____" puts out an opinion that takes people mentally into that opinion, and because of the permissive nature of this pattern, the subject tends to agree with your suggestion.

Persuasion Pattern 6:

VI.   I have a feeling _____

- Example: I have a feeling God's happiness is entering this place today.

- Purport: Feelings are kinesthetic—relating to touch and sensation. You can use this language pattern to suggest that someone is feeling a certain way, when talking to another person (group), and the feelings you suggest that person is feeling become transferred automatically to the person (group) you're talking to. This pattern can also be used less indirectly, and more directly, to suggest that someone will experience something or start to feel a certain way about something—for example, "I have a feeling God is going to bless you with a supernatural blessing after you bless the Kingdom of God with your first $1000.00 faith seed."

Persuasion Pattern 7:

VII.   Get a hold of this. _____

- Example: Get a hold of this. God loves you!

- Purport: This language pattern recaptures attention or intensifies the attention already held by your subject. It also intensifies the suggestion that comes immediately after; namely, making that suggestion more powerful. Consider the suggestion presented without the "Get a hold of this" part. Hear in your mind only, "God loves you!" Now ask yourself how you feel about that. Now, wait a minute or two, and consider: "Get a hold of this. God loves you!" and notice the difference. Pretty powerful difference, isn't there! The last thing to make you aware of is that the world "hold" is a kinesthetic word, affecting emotions, and so there is a direct association between the words "hold" and "love" in this statement.

Persuasion Pattern 8:

VIII.   I (you) cannot _____, until I (you) _____

- Example: You cannot enter the kingdom of heaven until you have confessed your sins.

- Purport: This is a cause effect pattern, in which you can make compelling assertions about anything you like. You can place emphasis through the use of tonality on words like "cannot" and "until" to make the sentence sound more imperative and to create a sense of urgency. People often will listen to a message, but without a sense of urgency (Holy Spirit talking to them) they won't take action as immediately. The more urgency in your message, the more urgent action taken by your subject. This is especially helpful when bringing people into Christianity (e.g., I **can-_not_** help you get saved, until you have faith in our Lord and Savior Jesus Christ. I **cannot**!).

Persuasion Pattern 9:

IX.　The more _____, the more _____

- Example: The more you attend church, the more wisdom God gives you—it is as simple as this!

- Purport: This cause effect pattern is very assumptive; that is, it creates an argument that must be acted upon in order to determine its efficacy. Until someone actually does something, you suggest they do, more often than they are doing it now, they cannot really argue the validity—in effect you get what you want; whether they do or not. Always use this and all persuasion patterns ethically and to promote the will of a just God.

Persuasion Pattern 10:

X.　When you _____, then you _____

- Example: When you are given an instruction by God, then you are bound until you carry forth that instruction.

- Purport: This persuasion pattern is, yet, another, cause effect pattern. The true beauty of this pattern is the logic-like foundation which can be created (e.g., When you listen to me, then you will understand!). Certainly, this isn't necessarily true; however, to find out the subject must listen to you. The presupposition that in order to realize what may very much be desired, requires first doing something you may not necessarily want to do, but which they assume is necessary, creates the case for them doing it—and in my experience—most people generally will. Just remember, they will, when it is their will, not necessarily because it's God's will. Of course you could say something like: "When you obey God's will, your willingness to move outside your comfort zone and experience life on a whole new level of faith immediately increases supernaturally!

What if You Apply these Persuasion Patterns?

If you apply these persuasion patterns to your preaching you'll begin to have a greater appreciation for language and make you're preaching much more compelling. These patterns take the guess work out of finding the right words to say to get your persuasive messages across to your subjects.

We come across people all the time who have a certain charisma about them, whose language seems to whisk us away into their world—separate from our own realities. Sometimes we find ourselves immersed in a wonder that's more enjoyable and exciting than our own dull lives. The adage: "We want what we can't have, and when we get it don't want it anymore," is true enough to make us seek something greater, where you find yourself in a completely different state. I want you to be able to take people on these types of journeys—it's what they want!

Imagine being able to use these patterns and noticing people bent on being in your company, driving home after church, and thinking about how blessed are they. You become that blessing for them. The message, God's message, carried through you, still lives on and affects people in ways unimaginable to us.

If you take the time to learn these patterns I'm sure you'll find other ways to use them, and ways of using them that inspire and uplift people. The experience is what you give when you preach using these patterns. Ask yourself: "What experiences do I want my subjects to have?"

The takeaway is this: you become great persuader and influencer of God's followers.

Chapter Summary

In this chapter you've learned about the Milton Model, Meta Model, and ten persuasion patterns. You've learned that language can be indirect and vague and still carry certain meanings. You've learned that human beings, when they communicate, do so deleting, distorting, and generalizing information—like they do when they perceive their map of reality through their limited senses. We all make generalizations based on our conditioning. We all delete experiences from our memory. We all distort or have a different recall of events and experiences we've had, because we all interpret and store information differently, based on our beliefs and ideas about how the world should be and what it is.

Our inner voice, or self-talk, is always talking; telling us what we're thinking and what we should be doing, etc. Through this process we're creating a limited reality in our minds, eschewing ideas and beliefs that do not work for us, and embracing those which do. Sometimes we act impulsively; sometimes we don't. Our decisions are a result of our mental states.

Persuasion patterns, you've learned, are linguistic patterns that can be adapted for any persuasion context. In this book that context is preaching. By memorizing these patterns you gain new resources to pull from your mental tool box, to help you be more persuasive and never have to search for words to say ever again.

Action Steps

The following actions steps are meant to help you bridge the great divide from theory to action. I've heard it said that 80% of self-help books never get read all the way through, and only 20% of people ever complete the action steps found at the end of each chapter. Maybe you've heard of the 80/20 rule:

> "So the 80/20 Principle states that there in an inbuilt imbalance between causes and results, inputs and outputs, and effort and reward."

—Richard Koch

In other words, 80% of the wealth winds up in the hands of 20% of the population. Twenty percent of products contribute to eighty percent of sales. This statistical discovery has been labeled Pareto's Law, after its founder, Italian economist, Vilfredo Pareto. Pareto in 1906 discovered that 80% of Italy's land was owned by 20% of the population. Significantly, this is found in economics, business, and many other disciplines to ring true; where 20% of some group will benefit from the efforts of the other 80% of the population of that group. These imbalances create leveraged opportunities for those willing to capitalize and do what the 20% does, while avoiding what the 80% doesn't do. I'm sure you can relate this back to one of our persuasion models if you go looking for it.

Suffice to say, I want you to be in the 20% of action takers and gain the true value of what I have to teach you. Certainly the choice is yours, and I'm not there to strike the back of your hands with a rule-stick; however, should you decide to pursue the true value, you'll gain the most, and realize the rewards that 80% percent of the readers won't. Not everyone will be truly great—will you?

I will be repeating this exact same intro to the action steps for each chapter. Do not be alarmed and think I'm doing it on accident to fill up pages. If I wanted to fill up pages, I'd increase the font size and double-space the lines, and add in a bunch of filler; I wouldn't do that to you! Remember back and recall the first words of chapter 1:

"Only what we keep hearing do we believe."

—*Bryan Westra*

I. Take a full day to listen to people and watch out for the abstract, vague, unclear, and indirect language patterns they use, and note mentally or on paper what those exact sentences are and then label them in terms of where they fall on the Milton Model. Doing this will teach you the Milton Model faster, and make you more perceptive to other people's language usage.

II.   Take day two to ask Meta Model violation questions to people who violate the various Meta Model categories, i.e. distortions, deletions, and generalizations. This will help you challenge beliefs and ideas people have that may not be useful anymore to them—or true.

III.   Take day three to practice using the persuasion patterns in all of your conversations with others. Notice how other people respond (e.g., non-verbal behavior, facial expressions, and what responses they give you back. Memorize the ten language patterns.

CHAPTER 3

The Language of Persuasion is God (Part 3)

A day goes by, and then another, and another. One day you wake-up with a different attitude; a different outlook on life. The beliefs you've believed in your past, about yourself, are diminished; while a moment of inspiration and heartfelt action is in order. You take on a new journey. What you've been afraid to do, you can't help but do. Your personal power is increased, and looking forward you will never be the same. It's a wake-up call.

What you couldn't do, you find yourself doing. What was impossible is now possible. You must take action—and, you do.

Before you know it, you're not the same person.

Before you die, you say a prayer. A prayer telling God how you've done your absolute best, and you thank Him for the best journey.

Your life on Earth is complete—you die.

At your funeral there are many people. People you know well, and people you've only had brief encounters with, and people who've only heard about you through other people. They are all telling stories about their experiences with you. They share their tears and choked smiles—all while reminiscing about your enormity and the positive impact you've made in their lives, your love toward them, and the person that you were in life.

You can probably see them, but maybe not, but it doesn't matter—you followed your heart and the Holy Spirit, and did what you needed to. You were blessed in countless measure and blessed so many in this way—by God for sure!

Now, I want to take you back to the present. Back to the pages of this book. Jump out of this story, because it is time to learn about the power of a story, and how you can use stories to inspire and influence people effortlessly.

We won't merely be covering stories in this chapter; rather, you'll be learning how to tell special types of stories—hypnotic stories—that influence and persuade your subjects. These stories make you extremely attractive—like a magnet.

When you get to the end of this chapter, you'll be able to deliver a story like a longtime, old school, professional storyteller. Your sermons will take on a whole new dimension. You'll be a force for good, and your charisma will elevate you to the place where only the best preachers sit. You'll be spell binding, and, best of all, you'll be helping your subjects improve their relationships with God in ways unimaginable.

There is one primary logical advantage that is in a class all its own when it comes to adding storytelling to your repertoire of persuasion resources; namely, gaining the ability to tell a story and fill any amount of time you need to. Let's say for some reason you somehow find yourself being invited on the spot to deliver a message to another church's congregation. Maybe the pastor there invites you up to the pulpit during the middle of a service; unbeknownst to you this was going to be requested beforehand. You're utterly shocked! You have nothing prepared to speak on. Your mind is a blank screen. There're people here expecting you to do something supernatural. The *only* thing needed, in such a rare event as this, is simply to tell a story. Nothing else.

There are several benefits to storytelling; namely: (a) stories indirectly relay a persuasive message, (b) stories transport people into new worlds, (c) stories create emotional convictions in the minds of the people listening, (d) stories make you, i.e. the storyteller, more interesting, (e) stories sell your message, (f) stories make people want to listen to you and come back Sunday after Sunday to hear more.

I'll be sharing with you many attributes of a mixture of storytelling models, and how you can adopt these models and tell stories on the fly automatically. I'll also cover some of the most common hang-ups many people have when it comes to telling stories; more exactly, to ensure you don't make these novice storytelling mistakes. Lastly we'll look into the indirectness of storytelling and explore some of the parables of Jesus, and how Jesus told stories.

The Success Story

Everyone loves a happy ending. The Success Story always ends on a positive note; that is, a happy ending. A simple story like The Success Story begins with an ordinary situation, which builds to a climax, and then finds a resolution. The Success Story starts with something ordinary in the way of a main character, and quickly if not instantly this character realizes some dilemma or problem. The climax is at this realization, and also when the character is faced with an "us versus them" situation. At some point down the line the conflict is ended when a successful solution is found. Very often these types of stories utilize repurposing to take a seemingly unimportant detail and later toward the end of the story making it purposeful. Let's explore this story model in more detail, shall we?

Why the Success Story?

A success story is a very simple to tell, which has a really great message; namely, something seemingly negative turns out to be a positive. Already you are forming some type of impression or recollection in your mind about this type of story. One problem most people new to storytelling run into is where to start, and once they finally get started, where to go next. Notice that I've already given you a mental blueprint about the story's direction before I've actually told you a story. I've done this to solve this core problem most people have when they're going to tell a story, i.e. the problem of where to start, and what to say next. So just having a mental template about such a simple story, you can more easily pick a starting point and carry your story forward until you finish. Another benefit to solving this problem in this way is that you're freed-up to embellish your story and add more details to make it a richer more captivating story.

What is the Success Story?

The Success Story begins with a problem. It doesn't matter necessarily what that problem is—depending on the context and audience any problem will do. It is, let me say, better if you can relate your story as closely as you can with your audience. Food for thought.

For our purposes, let's assume that our main character's name is John, and John has a problem—he's lost his car keys from partying at the bar the night before.

Next, the main character goes in search for a solution to the problem. They're searching out a solution in all directions—obsessively focused on finding the solution. Not thinking about much else.

Again for our purposes, let's say that John is searching everywhere around his house for those keys. He's calling up friends he went out drinking with to ask them how he got home and to see if any of them has his keys.

Next, the main character runs into a confrontation with someone else; someone who is negatively affected by the problem John has caused for himself.

Back to our example, let's assume John's father is upset because John's car is parked behind his truck, and now his father cannot get out of the driveway and it caused him to miss his job for the entire day. John's father is irate and chastising John for being so irresponsible.

The next part requires a solution. A solution is a resolve or an event that happens in the story to solve the problem.

In our example, let's assume that the fix to John's missing keys problem is the spare set his mother, who lives across town, who is divorced from John's father, has in her possession. Let's assume, since neither John nor his father can leave to pick up the keys so his mother agrees to drop them by John's father's house.

Let's stop for just a moment. I want you to consider already, and I bet you already have, what they outcome of this story will be. Do you have it? Think about this question: How would you end the story, given the details I've just presented to you? Okay... Let's go on...

The next attribute to The Success Story is a surprise or shock. For John this could be his father sharing with John how he quit his job, when his tyrant of a boss called him irresponsible on the phone earlier. John's shocked by this news and delighted when his father apologizes, and tells John how much better off he is not that he's finally called it quits with that terrible boss—a boss he blames for his failures as a father and former husband.

The last attribute to this story is the problem getting solved. One great way of making the ending more powerful is through repurposing earlier parts of the story, which seemed minor if not insignificant into the conclusion of the story.

So in our example, let's say John's mother comes by, and is invited into John's father's house, and rekindles her love for John's father, upon hearing the news he's quit his job, and has a new lease on life.

It is a happy ending, right? Certainly, because John has gotten a wakeup call that partying too much equals loss of consciousness which leads to loss of car keys, or in his mind, perhaps even worst consequences. This may be a moral lesson not to be irresponsible or to drink to get drunk. Furthermore, John's father realizes the lesson that working so much that you exclude people you care about from your life, results in an unbalanced life that you hate. Finally, the family is brought back together under rather strangely bizarre circumstances that becomes the best possible solution for all characters involved.

Now ask yourself how much effort, do you think, I put into telling you that story. The answer might surprise you. The answer is I put zero effort into telling that story, and I made it up completely on the fly. How was I able to do this? Using the template I've just given you for The Success Story.

How to Tell a Success Story?

To make this easier I've decided to give you a basic outline that you can use as a cheat sheet. This cheat sheet will help you master the few quick steps necessary to tell The Success Story.

    I.   Start with a problem (e.g., lost keys)

    II.   Search for a solution (e.g., frantic tearing up the house)

    III.   Us versus Them (e.g., John against his father)

IV.   Find solution (e.g., John remembered his mother has a spare set)

V.   Surprise or shock (e.g., John's problem caused his father to quit)

VI.   Problem solved (e.g., happy ending – John's mother and father re-
kindle their love for each other and the family is reunited back)

So this is The Success Story. Now you have six basic attributes that make this story work to bring home the point. To illustrate this in the context of preaching, let me present you with another story.

There is a man who has been sentenced to die on a cross next to Jesus. This man is guilty for his crime, but the problem is he's still got to die. On the cross, he's up there contemplating his pain, and knows it is just a matter of time before he will die. There's nobody who will save him. Up there he's taken aback, shocked, if you will, by this personality he's heard so much about—this person Jesus—who claims to be the Son of God. Left with nothing to lose and everything to gain he accepts Jesus Christ as his Lord and Savior, while up there on the cross beside him, and Jesus offers him eternal salvation. When the man dies he enters the kingdom of heaven, and all because of an unfortunate circumstance he found himself in. Had it not been for his sins, punishment, and accepting Jesus as God, he would likely not have entered the kingdom. In heaven, the man enjoys supreme happiness.

What if You Adopt this Model Into Your Preaching?

I want you to think for a few minutes about the implication of telling similar Success Stories while you preach. Do you think this would engage your audience? Do you think it would draw people into the story?

What about the persuasive implication? Don't tell dry facts; rather, tell your subjects feel good, emotionally laden stories, and you'll instantly experience your subjects wanting to hear more, instead of wishing the service was over.

You might want to consider ways you can make your story relevant to the biblical message you want relayed. If, for example, you are trying to get through the point that it is better to be satisfied, appreciative, grateful, and blessed feeling with what one already has; rather, than focused on always wanting more and more material possessions—you might want to include the story of Adam and Eve and the temptation that led to sin and death for all humankind. This is a biblical; however, to make your message more modern and relevant to today's generation, you might want to tell a story about a time when you were tempted and how it caused a huge problem for you. You may want to expound on the details, and share how the temptation led to some positive outcome resolving the problem.

Why you might want to include a story that more or less parallels the Adam and Eve story, is because it is likely most of your subjects have read this story and/or heard it told numerous times. A story they haven't heard, instantly elevates the affects preaching has on your subjects, since it's something new and something they can empathize with you on. It also conveys your human nature and contrasts human qualities everyone has.

The Hypnotic Story

In this model, the use of indirect conversational hypnosis is employed to make your storytelling irresistible and ultra-compelling—moreover more effective in persuading and captivating your audience. This is actually a highly advanced form of storytelling that requires some practice and understanding to do it effectively. Once you master this ability you'll have achieved the rarest storytelling abilities.

The hypnotic story leverages the persuasion technique of the Zeirgarnik Effect; that is, a psychological principle. Now, the Zeirgarnik Effect is the tendency that an individual has to experience some rather intrusive thoughts about a particular objective, which the individual once pursued, but which was left incomplete. Let me give you an example of how the Zeirgarnik Effect works, which will give you a better idea about what it is actually.

To exemplify, let me share a personal account. As of writing this book I have recently put on hold another book I was in the process of completing. This book project was one that I was well near completion, but due to more research and a necessary delay, I have left the project on hold for now. I did not want to post pone this book, so I decided to begin it, while I wait for some externalities to catch up to let me complete the other book.

Since putting the project on hold, my conscious mind has consistently thought about that project, and have felt dissonance having not completed it yet. The mental experience I have encountered is categorically known as the Zeigarnik Effect. It's interesting. I haven't been able to get the book out of my head, and I feel a tendency to want to work on the project mentally all the time. It has caused me anxiety in fact.

The next book I work on after this one will, for this reason, be that incomplete book project. I continually think about the research needed, which will actually require international travel to India, to finalize it. I have to wait on confirmation of some research outlets to open up first, but suffice to say, I'll finish that book before I start another.

Something left incomplete is comparable, in my mind, to someone who suffers from Obsessive Compulsive Disorder (OCD) who will not be able to focus on anything else in their life fully until they feel right about the placement of something in their home, or undergo some ritual. In my mind, it is sort of the same. I haven't been able to satisfy my mind, as I know I still have this looming project over my head, waiting for me to complete it.

So really what the Ziergarnik Effect is the dissonance of having something incomplete. In storytelling this happens sometimes. You'll be listening to someone tell you a story and then for some obscure reason, they have to stop and proceed onto other activities—for example, their cell phone rings and they're called off to do something, leaving you guessing about the end of the story. You cannot get the thought out of your head. Try as you may you experience this lingering affective state where you desperately wanting to know the ending. It is the only way you will gain peace.

The interesting thing to note about the Ziergarnik Effect is that the discomfort and anxiety can go on forever. You can have been told a story and will face the dissonance until which time the outcome is learned. So this is a very powerful psychological phenomenon that happens. It's one that, if used practically, in the art of storytelling, can be very useful and very hypnotic in its affect.

When the conscious mind is focused on the outcome of what one story's ending should be, another story can actually have begun, and the listener's conscious mind is so focused on what they haven't discovered yet that they are distracted from the next story being told. When this happens embedded commands and persuasive patterns can be implanted in the new story which go undetected by the conscious mind of the subject and directly into the other mind; resulting in the post-hypnotic suggestions being carried out automatically. Your subject will not even be cognizant of the fact they've been given a hypnotic suggestion. They will not know why they're doing the things they're doing. They will assume it's their own idea and that the reason they are doing it is because they're choosing to do it. You'll know otherwise.

To teach you this model I will have to teach you how to plant a hypnotic suggestion in your subject's mind. After you learn this model, you notice as you watch some of the best preachers, that they'll be using this approach to storytelling while delivering their sermons.

It is imperative that you understand that just because you can always get what you want, doesn't mean you should. In other words—be ethical as to how you use these covert persuasion methods. You should only suggest to people things which will help them. Do not use this approach for your own ends, forgetting about your own faith in God, and your own moral principles. If you do, bad things will likely happen to you as a result. I don't want that for you, and I don't want people being covertly influenced by you for the fun of it or to manipulate them into doing things that are detrimental to them and others. Please, please, please, head my warning.

With that out of the way, let's start learning, shall we...?

Why You Need to Learn Hypnotic Storytelling?

Besides the fact that everybody who is anybody in preaching circles, who have made a living off of influence and persuasion tactics, and who has mastered some of the skills used in conversational hypnosis and hypnotic storytelling. You want to learn hypnotic storytelling to simply improve your everyday communications—to make the stories you tell count; that is, more compelling and interesting and attractive to your listening audience.

When you learn how to tell hypnotic stories using the formula I'll be teaching you here, you'll be able to influence and persuade subjects in a way they won't even know they're being persuaded or influenced to do something you want them to do. In fact, the person being influenced will simply appreciate your good humor and your witty ability to tell stories in such a insightful way that they just simply cannot help but want to be around you and do the things you want them to do. What will seem like an arbitrary story will actually be a secret front to induce persuasion.

Another reason why you want to learn how to tell hypnotic stories is because it is everywhere you look around you. I mean just think about a most recent movie which came out you watched, which completely captivated you. When we go back to the Narrative Transportation Theory, one of our psychological models of persuasion, we're reminded of the fact that stories have the tendency to take people and drop them into different states of mind and have them empathetic to certain characters which are figments of someone else's imagination. Even in their minds, they will be taking on the role of the main character or sub characters.

Hollywood and Bollywood have mastered the art of storytelling. These screenplays are written to sell movies—they are spellbinding and extremely hypnotic. The reason people buy movies or books of fiction is because people simply enjoy being taken into a different world beyond they reality they live in. It also seems safe for them to engage in a movie; rather, engaging in some actual event. Entering a movie is done so with the expectation that the watcher will be the same when the movie is over. Oftentimes this isn't the case; rather, people will be changed, only to not know it. I mean think about it. People live in everyday normal situations which can be boring to the bone. Sometimes an escape seems like a good idea, even preferred; people need a different experience to see contrast to what they have.

By giving people an outlet to navigate into a different reality we open up possibilities for them. We make them aware of things they otherwise wouldn't have been aware of. I mean, if there's ideas or suggestions that you want them to consider, by putting them into a different state of mind or altogether different reality, they take on the behavior of the characters and the tendencies the characters would portray in a certain situational context. By vicariously living in that character's shoes through the story, so to speak, they essentially will naturally want to do and take the same courses of action that a character would likely do. So stories are very, very, important to ministry. They are very important to preaching in general. These are all some of the reasons you'd want to assert stories into your preaching messages.

When you learn how to tell stories eloquently and in a way that people cannot help but want to be around you, you take on a new power you didn't have before. I find it very interesting that you can learn one thing and learn it well and it can completely change your entire range of abilities. It is the same way with story-telling and persuasion; namely, when you learn how to tell stories, in the way I'll be teaching you how, you'll be able to literally have people at your beckon call. They will want to hear your stories; fictional or your real life accounts recounted.

I invite you into this section on hypnotic storytelling for the purpose of taking people outside their small dot of a reality and expand their experiences to the outer periphery of the world they live in mentally—into altogether new realities they've not experience before.

When I was in my teenage years, I became fascinated by historical figures and their biographies. I remember on time covering a small section on Indian history; specifically, how it related to India's partition, and the man named Mohandas Gandhi. Gandhi was a non-violent activist, who helped contribute to the exit of British rule, making India a self-governing democratic nation.

"I am prepared to die, but there is no cause for which I am prepared to fight. Truth and non-violence are my God." —M.K. Gandhi

Gandhi was a very influential and persuasive personality. He was able to influence people by his actions, and cause them to rethink their ideologies. He even won the honor, "Man of the Millennium" in Time Magazine. I, personally, was influenced by his persuasive abilities and the values he was willing to die for, if need be. I wanted to, as a child, learn more about him.

The Internet was in its infancy in those days. Gathering information wasn't near as easy as it is today, because we didn't have Google Search, or other search engines for that matter; like we do today! Finding information was challenging. It was sometimes a matter of luck, and typing in the right URL and hoping to uncover what we sought to uncover.

I was walking one day to a college bookstore. They had outside the bookstore a rack of books they were trying to get rid of. These books were part of their collection that wasn't that popular.

I'm looking on this rack, and before I enter, I see Gandhi's autobiography. I see it's only .25 cents. Being a poor college student, I rarely had extra money to buy a book for pleasure reading, as I spent so much on required text books—not to mention I didn't have much time to read non-required reading in those days.

Because the book was inexpensive I bought it that day. I began reading it that afternoon, and did not put the book down until I was completely finished reading the whole book.

This one book had such a profound impact on my thinking. It totally changed my values and perception on life. I was extremely influenced by the persuasion in the book.

I tell you this because the affect one book had on me personally brought me into a whole new reality; namely, a reality that inspired me to learn more about non-violence and how people should be treated by other people.

From this life-altering experience I eventually found myself in India. Through a series of serendipitous events I astonishingly found myself interviewing one of the men responsible for killing Gandhi. His name was Gopal Godse.

So this gave me an utterly different perspective; countering what I had learnt about Gandhi in his autobiography.

I conducted an interview and shared a meal with Gopal Godse, and it was a very special moment in my life to be able to get this unique perspective on why he killed Gandhi and his feelings on the partition of what today is two separate countries, i.e. India and Pakistan. This was a rare account, and today Godse is dead, so I count myself fortunate to have been able to pursue this to its ends.

I can say that from buying a .25 cent book, I made a journey that was unimaginable and which gave me an experience like no other. It was the best .25 cents I've ever spent. This is the power of a story, and why you need to learn about hypnotic storytelling—it can be very impactful.

As a side note: When we use the word hypnotic or hypnosis we're simply alluding to how people become mesmerized or captivated or that one's attention is completely focused; rather, it's not about any metaphysical woo-woo or anything that goes against your own Christian ideals and beliefs. It is simply a state of mind where one become transported into the pages of a book and into a different reality altogether. Much like being emotionally affected when reading a story from the Bible or a movie on Christ's crucifixion.

I think another way you may want to consider hypnotic storytelling is from the analogy of telling young children fairytales. These fables are put forward to teach a moral lesson or indoctrinate children about the values of obeying their parents, avoiding dangers, and the consequences which occur when these lessons are not learnt. It is easier to remember a story's essence; that is, it's thread of wisdom and meaning, than it is to remember a parent's lecture. In olden days these tales were highly effective in persuading children to do right and not wrong.

With this in mind, let's turn to what we need to understand about hypnotic storytelling to be able to tell these powerfully persuasive stories effectively to achieve our desired end result.

What You Need to Learn About Hypnotic Storytelling?

What you really need to understand about hypnotic storytelling is that all stories are hypnotic to some degree. What we're doing when we tell hypnotic stories in the way I'll be teaching you is taking the reader or listener deeper and deeper into the story to the extent they actually forget what they're doing and where we actually in many ways shut down the conscious barriers so that the individual can become completely immersed in the story.

See, some stories may have some persuasive affect mentally on the reader or listener; however, it may be only a small affect. It could be an affect which causes them to mildly engage with the story or to get something from it. It could be that they get something meaningful or some takeaway that is later recalled and which might have some usefulness to them. Or it could be something as simple as a joke told to lighten the mood. This joke can later be retold by the subject to someone else—this creates a viral marketing effect, where your message reaches others indirectly. The benefits of this could be more church attendance and more people coming to the Lord. Telling a humorous story that can be easily remembered and retold; rather, would make it easier for your subjects to share Christ's message to others. Anytime you can make it easier for your sheep to share the gospel's good news with others is definitely a positive for your ministry and those brought into the Christian fold.

Oftentimes these jokes and puns are great ice breakers. They help to build rapport with your audience. Humor is also used in advertising with great result. You'll, for example, see a 30 second commercial on television where humor is employed, utilizing these funny skits and seemingly ridiculous storylines. These can be notions that take the viewing audience into the commercial subtly associating the humor to the brand they are promoting.

If we revisit the respondent conditioning model we see why humor is employed in these ads. It is because of the anchors associated with the humor and the brand. When consumers visit retail stores to buy a brand, the brand triggers unconscious association with humor; namely, an emotional state in which people more often buy items. These associations are unconscious and beneath the radar of cognition, thereby making them powerful influencers. This explains as buyers why we sometimes wonder why we've made a purchase, after a purchase has been made. It is subliminal associations like these that can very easily and covertly be integrated into storytelling. The attitude a brand has in our psyche is created through these associations, intensifying the goodwill and intrinsic value a particular brand has to us as consumers. This is why we may but the expensive brand over the generic brand. They may be the same exact product but one carries a greater intrinsic value than the other—and so we buy that one.

When we tell deeper hypnotic stories, like the ones I'll be teaching you, you can definitely incorporate any type of story into this system and make it work; so long as the story is tasteful and congruent with context and your subject's expectations. In other words, if you're talking about the positive facets of Islam to a dominantly Christian audience you may get the rotten tomatoes thrown at you, so to speak. So you definitely want to make sure that you are congruent with the types of messages and stories you're delivering to your audience. As anyone in publishing or public speaking will tell you, always keep your audience in mind and appeal to their self-interests.

"Be willing to try new ideas and always keep the reader in mind. Our readers are 21st-century kids who live in a multiplatform world, who want fun and excitement,

as well as the timeless quality of a good story."—Ellie Berger, President of Trade Publishing

You want to be wise and listen to other people tell stories. You may want to actually keep a journal of stories that have affected you in some way, and make a note of the affect. Doing this will give you a lot of stories to draw from when needed. The best part of this strategy is that you'll already know in general sense what affect the story will have on your audience, because you know already what affect it has had on you. Stories can be retold in your own flavor, making them uniquely yours, only the general storyline attributed to someone else. There are millions and millions of stories out there to be borrowed, cleaned up, and customized to use as you want. Stories are told every day, and chances are by the end of today, you'll have either listened to a story being told, or told a story yourself; chances are, I bet you experience both, and countless times. Repurposing for you own purposes is a powerful way to tell stories, therefore keep this in mind.

What you also need to understand are some of the fundamentals of the hypnotic storytelling model. Here are some of those components I'll be teaching you how about and sharing with you how you can integrate them into your stories to make your stories that much more powerful:

- Nested loop pattern: We tell a story and 2/3^{rds} through just before the climax, using the Zeirgarnik principle, stop the story and begin another story. We then repeat this process until we've finished our last story, and then loop back around and close the loop in reverse order. There are hard brakes (e.g., instantly drop one story and begin anew) and there are soft brakes (e.g., subtly shift into a new story unsuspectingly). The stories can be related stories or completely different stories. Since the conscious mind can only focus on 7+/- 2 bits of information at any given time, the critical faculty is caught off guard, and the unconscious o other mind is open to suggestions you'll be directly planting in your subject's mind.

- Hypnotic themes: These are the emotional essence of your story or point you want to get across—for example, fear, anger, relaxation, excitement, love, happiness, exuberance, etc. Things that make an individual experience specific emotional states used for having them to want to and actually take certain types of actions when provoked or suggested to do so.

- Emotionally laden words: These words utilize specific words to create specific states in your subjects, to produce specific results. These create the type of behavior you want out of your subjects—for example, "excitement". Excitement is a buying state. You want to sell something, first get someone excited. People get excited about buying things—shopping an exciting experience in and of itself. When someone falls in love, and get excited about the prospects of the relationship, they tend to buy gifts, and do not mind spending money on the gifts, because they're excited and happy to do so. The buyer's remorse only happens when the other person dumps you, and then you want your stuff back. Recalling our psychological persuasion models this of course is the cognitive dissonance model of persuasion. A lot of money is made when and where people are excited. If you get your congregation excited about Jesus, surely they'll want to donate more to the offering plate.

- Extended quotes: These we have covered back when we learnt the Milton Model. This is when you quote something someone else has said, which you yourself really wanted to say. When you say it chances are it isn't true; when someone else says it, it must be true. When we're telling hypnotic stories we utilize these to give a suggestion and make it more buyable in the mind of the subject. For example, "My friend John Doe told me that he was going to town to buy a new car, because the dealership across town offered the best deals this week." See how this might persuade a potential buyer to want to go and check out the dealership. These work.

- Embedded commands: These are suggestions or commands made inside a story, but which only get picked up by the unconscious or other mind of the subject. These suggestions are marked out using a process known as analogue marking. When you teach people *buy this product* it works wonders in your favor. ← Analogue marked suggestion ("but this product").

- Persuasion patterns: These are the ten patterns we learned earlier, which help influence and persuade your subject to take action. We'll be adding these to our stories to make them more hypnotically compelling and persuasive.

- Sensory system predicates: These are words that correlate with the five senses. Using a variety of these helps to better create the mental image of the story in your subject's mind—for example: Get a hold of this (kinesthetic), and listen to what I'm about to tell you (auditory), because once you see what's in store (visual) you'll quickly realize the smell of fresh crisp one hundred dollar bills (olfactory) and can't you just taste the sweet rewards that will be happening like domino effect (gustatory)?

- Awareness predicates: These are words that focus awareness and direct it where you want it to go—for example: aware, visualize, think, understand, believe, notice, imagine, recall, focus, etc.

- Syntax: This means word order in a sentence. Some sentences are passive while others are much more direct, and it all depends on word order. For instance: "He bought the cow," versus "The cow was bought by him." The first is quite direct, while the second is much more passive; however, take note, because they both are relaying essentially the same message. Simply rearranging a sentence can create a completely different effect in a subject's mind.

We'll also be looking at stories on a larger level, and then move onto the Monomyth in the next section of this chapter. So these are some of the things you need to understand and things we'll be covering in greater detail when we transition next into the "how" of creating hypnotic stories.

How to Tell a Hypnotic Story?

The hypnotic story, much like the simple story, has a basic structure to it. To break this structure down into its simplest form what we're going to do is start an even or a routine. During this event or routine as some point we're then going to interrupt it in some way. It can be any type of interruption. The more interesting your story becomes depends on how mindboggling the interruption. The further away from normal you get usually the more compelling your story becomes; however, if you make your story too interrupted by some very strange and unbelievable event the critical faculty tends to raise a red flag to your conscious mind. This is usually where people start to make some type of assertion as to whether or not the story if fiction or nonfiction.

With a hypnotic story I have found and I have witnessed from the sermons I've listened to, and the research that I've done that a really good hypnotic story usually borders somewhere in between fiction and nonfiction. The reason for this is that you want to have some amount of confusion and some question as to is this story real or is it just a made up tale. For example, if you're telling a story about a young man who's been driving down the interstate and several hours have gone by and then all of a sudden, out of the blue, an alien zaps him up to outer space, the listener will probably start to immediately acknowledge that this is a fictitious story. If you are the listener (subject) this story is completely fiction; there is no way in the world that an alien is going to zap someone up to outer space.

Now if you were to tell your story: A young man was driving down the interstate and several hours had passed and all of a sudden he looked over and he saw that there had been a major car accident. You could see the burn vehicles from the blaze. Then this is something that is relatable. This is something that rings of non-fiction, but it doesn't have to be. So you're sort of left wondering. The more details you have about the character—for example, the name of the character, the type of car being driven, the exact location, etc.—the more likely you are to begin to develop clues about whether this is a story of fiction or non-fiction.

So these are type of stories you want to tell. You want to keep your stories plausible. I think plausible is a really good word for it, because it could happen, but maybe not. These types of stories really land the listener's ears back; that is to say, pin them back and make them alert like a radar searching for something to show up out of the blue, unexpected. People listening to these types of stories become intrigued and really want to make sense of the storyline. There's a great mystery that needs to be solved.

Maybe an even better story could be: There's a young man driving down the interstate. He has been for several hours. He's fatigued physically and mentally. He's yawning more and more. Rubbing his eyes unconsciously. All of a sudden, out of the blue, something darts across the highway. It flew by so fast the young man almost missed seeing it. In his mind, the young man thought, "This must be a half-invisible thing, or animal, or something or other."

So you see that in this last story there's something in the middle. There's not the obvious fiction of an alien. There's also not the accident that happens every day on some major highway in America. Now we have a half-invisible creature thingy darting across the highway. It raises instant questions. What was it? Was it anything at all? Is the young man's mind playing tricks on him? Was it most likely a sprinting deer, caught in the sunlight where it was difficult to make out exactly what was it? Is this story fiction or nonfiction? It raises a lot of intrigue. These types of stories suck in the reader. The young man is definitely relatable. There are aspect of his experience we all can relate with, because we've all, most likely, experienced a long drive, when we were half tired, and uncomfortable in the seat, doing our best to stay awake and alert, but wishing more than anything that we were already at our destination.

Now we're left guessing what exactly was going on? What exactly the young man actually seeing? We're checking in our memory banks, going back in what in NLP we call a Transderivational Search (TDS), to make meaning of this. To be able to understand it logically—a place we've been to before which is similar. We're looking at the young man's experience based on our own past experiences. This is very, very, powerful because people start to wonder, while their minds start to wander deeper and deeper into the story. All in all it becomes a very hypnotic evanescent experience taking place as the story is being told; yet, paradoxically, there's a lingering affect that keeps the subject going back to the story over and over, wondering what the ending should have been. This is the power of the Zeirgarnik effect, where we seek closure to something that has been started, and will stop at nothing until we find that meaning—the story then controls us.

So the next step is someone has to change, i.e. a character in the story changes. Note that when a character in the story changes, the subject mentally assuming the role of the character, also changes. This is one reason stories are powerful vehicles for change. This means someone is emotionally affected by some type of surreal experience. This could be where we start to insert various hypnotic themes; such as, emotions like anger, fear, love, and happiness. These are they type of feel-good or very extreme emotions that people tend to have, where they start to really change their mentality or mindset. They start to change their state, and you can see their body language shift, and their physiology start to change as well. When you're telling your story, and this change starts to happen it could be something very relatable. Oftentimes, when you're telling your story, you will be relating to your audience in some manner or other, often indirectly. This is what's so beautiful about these stories; they are so indirect and yet they do cause someone to experience emotions they haven't experienced in a long time. It gets to the core of human nature. When you start to get to the core of human nature, and what makes us human, and what separates us from other beings in terms of our abilities to feel certain emotions. These emotions could be ones like anger, fear, love, compassion, etc.

When people experience such emotions we start to see the best and worst sides of humanity. These are sides of our own personality; that is, the best and worst aspects of ourselves. In persuasion, of course, people do their best to avoid pain and embrace pleasure. Most people do not want to confront their own dark side, while they much prefer to engage with the positive side of their nature. Stories, open up the floodgates of possibility; indirectly making it possible to associate a character to emotional parts, safely letting us explore what we otherwise might wish not to.

These can be the ignorant, intolerance; these types of negatively charged emotions which alert us to who we don't want to be outwardly or for that matter even inwardly. These are the monster or demon aspects of ourselves. The sinful nature of humankind can affect us deeply. These changes, these emotionally affected, changes, inside someone, through an experience happening through this story, can very powerfully make people susceptible to experiencing or assuming you the speaker are talking directly to them—you are talking to an aspect of them which they are associating with through your story.

Our last step, and this certainly is optional, but it is something that is so powerful, and what I'm talking about is repurposing an earlier even or routine in the story into your ending, to make sense out of something earlier thought to be innocuous. This reincorporation it is very elegant; namely, as it relates to having your story come full-circle, so you can tell these very eloquent stories to your subjects. Usually, these seemingly useless details that have people feeling as though your story is very great, and it makes you the storyteller appear brilliant.

This is the basic hypnotic story structure. We start with an event. The event or routine is interrupted. Then someone is changed and emotionally affected by some experience that suddenly happens. Lastly, we repurpose something originally thought to be needless or innocuous and then reincorporate it back into our story to give it a purpose. It is the details of a story that make it truly great. The next part of our hypnotic story equation is to do just that—make our stories truly great by layering into our stories some very hypnotic details. First we must learn about nested loops, and from that base, we'll start adding in all the hypnotic details which will make your stories terrific, able to capture the hearts and minds of your subjects. Let's begin.

Nested Loops & the Zeirgarnik Effect

Nested loop patterns are when you begin telling a story and then somewhere near the climax, usually around 2/3rds of the way through your story, what you'll do is break the story off, using either a hard or a soft loop break. A hard break is an abrupt end, where another story, completely different, begins. A soft break is really a subtle shift from one story into the next story; a fade-in to the next story, and it could be something relatable to the original story. Maybe it's the storyteller who gets an insight while telling the first story to where s/he sort of leaves off telling that story and starts to very subtly and indirectly begin telling another story.

This is essentially what you're going to do. You're going to take one story and tell it, and when you get 2/3rds of the way through you're going to break it somehow and begin telling another story. You're going to tell that story until you get about 2/3rds of the way through; where the climax would be nearing, and you're going to break it again. Then, as before, you'll tell another story, and another, until you've told between 5 – 12 stories. If you start to tell any more than 12 stories it gets a little hairy, i.e. complicated, because it becomes challenging to remember the stories that you've told which have preceded the stories before. If you tell less than 5, perhaps the effect of what you're wanting isn't going to be as powerful in effect, and so really you probably want to tell a minimum of five stories. This does take time. It also takes practice. The more time and practice you have under your belt, the better storyteller you'll become. Soon, it will become an unconscious act whereby you'll tell stories without even realizing it, but in the way I've trained you to do, much the same way you probably naturally tell stories at random now.

Once you get to the last story. Say for example you've told five stories in this manner of breaking them at roughly 2/3rds of the way through. Now we get to the fifth and what we're going to do is complete this story, instead of breaking it. Once this is accomplished you'll then go back to the story just before the fifth one, so story four, and complete the loop, finishing this story. You'll then work backward all the way through until you get to story one. So after finishing story four, you'll finish story three, then you'll back to story number two, and finish it, then you'll go back to the very first story you began telling, story number one, and finish it.

What this does is creates, as we're telling the stories, a Zeirgarnik effect every time we break a story. This Zeirgarnik effect is where the mind is left wondering what's coming next. It becomes so focused on what's coming next, that it becomes truly difficult for the mind to focus on the next story, and the next story, and the next story.

To give you an idea of how the Zeirgarnik effect is used often in persuasion preaching, just consider the end of a televangelism program. Note the preacher often says, "Not now, but in a minute, after we pray, I'm going to ask you to go to the phones and phone in a thousand dollar seed. Not now, but in a minute. So do not call in now. First we're going to pray." The reason the preacher says it like this is for two reasons. One is it creates the Zeirgarnik effect, which has people unable to focus away from what they're being called to do. When the preacher is praying, the congregation is not hearing the prayer, but rather their inner voice is thinking about calling in. This gives the pastor time to deliver one last time the covert embedded commands which hypnotically persuade his/her congregation to do what he is asking them to do, through the guise of prayer. The second reason is that it presupposes that the congregation is going to do something after something else has been given. This is the influence principle of reciprocity—when I give you something (i.e., a prayer for your success and happiness) you then owe me something back in return (i.e., a thousand dollar seed). The brilliance of this technique is that it's forcing indebtedness with God, and not a person. It is, in other words, presupposed that God is going to give you something, so now you have to pay in return something back to God.

Now that you know how to tell a hypnotic story, and you've learned how to take those stories and chain-link them together using the nested loop pattern, it is time to learn how to install the details we talked about before.

Hypnotic Particulars that Animate Your Stories

The first layer I want you to begin to think about incorporating into your hypnotic stories are hypnotic themes. From a hypnotherapeutic context these themes would be suggestions like relaxation, comfort, and those types of things. These are useful for helping the psychotherapist's client to relax and have an easier time undergoing hypnosis. However, for our purposes here, because our context is preaching, our themes could be love, happiness, extreme excitement, purpose, drive, intention, recognition, abundance, and so on and so forth. We want to incorporate these themes into our stories—for example, if we have five different stories we may have a common thread running through all five encompassing one or more of these themes. The affect would be the same, it wouldn't seem out of place, it wouldn't raise any red flags to a person's conscious mind, meaning the listener would be getting dose after dose of this common theme repeating itself. Remember that only what we keep hearing do we believe. This is a common theme throughout this book. If you remember back to chapter one the very first sentence is this. In our stories we're doing the exact same thing, constantly repeating what we want people to believe. This is the secret to Christianity as I see it. The message has been repeated so much and so often that generation after generation more and more believers come into the Christian fold. This is why missionary activity is so effective, as we're ministering the Word of God to people everywhere all the time. Whenever someone discovers God they are acquiring access to everything that has come before—all the ground word other Christians have put forward generation after generation.

This common thread that's running through all of these stories would be very much like type of storyteller, and perhaps you've heard them before, where they start to tell one story, and suddenly lose track of that story, and start on a completely different story. It's really the free flow of ideas that happen naturally when people tell stories without even thinking about it. The only difference here is that we're actually putting it into a structure and we're actually intentionally telling our stories.

So we want to tell these stories as close to telling them like a real conversation would happen so that they don't raise any suspicion and all so that as we're starting to implant certain embedded commands into our stories throughout in which our subjects don't really understand what we're doing. There are certain parts of storytelling which remain completely secretive; namely, parts where we're not only increasing people's emotions intentionally, we're also giving those direct and indirect commands when we tell our stories. These are suggestions that influence decision making.

Turning our attention now to emotionally laden language –and, this emotionally laden language, these are hot-words, essentially. They invoke certain types of automatic responses through classical or respondent conditioning. We talked about respondent conditioning when we covered our persuasion models, if you recall. People are anchored to respond in kind to certain stimuli. The experiment conducted by Ivan Pavlov where he conditioned dogs to salivate to want to experience food when hearing a tuning fork or a bell. It is essentially the same thing that we're doing. Certain words, for example, in our human vocabulary have different intensities, and so it's your job as a preacher and a highly skilled communications expert to really start and become aware of these types of hot words. These hot words could be the different between a 'baby' versus an 'infant'. The baby has a much different connotation to us emotionally than what an infant does. An infant is more or less, it could be any infant, we're more detached from it, and less associated to it, and more dissociated in fact from it. Whereas a baby has a characteristic of like, "Oh. It's a baby!" A baby is something that is special whereas an infant is something that you might read about in a newspaper. The reason for these hot emotional words, the reason we're so conditioned to certain ones on higher frequencies, and not others, is because when we're very young, when we're learning our first vocabulary words, the words that were the simplest; namely, like 'baby' and various color preferences we learnt, and all these different types of things, these early words had the most impact on us emotionally. At an early age we were more emotionally susceptible to what's going on in the world around us. We're attached to our mothers and we have respect for our fathers and the world is a perfect bubble that we live in. At this age we're sheltered from the evils from the world, and so the things that come into our realities at that time have a very emotionally stimulating effect on us all the way throughout the rest of our lives. These are what sort of make up these hot words that act as emotional triggers sending us into certain states of mind.

As you're drafting out your sermons you need to keep in mind certain words are going to have certain influences on the psyche of your audience. These are the types of things we really want to zero in on. We want to start to use these inside our stories, to bring to life our stories, and more effectively transport our listener or subject rather into our stories—making them like a part of them and something unforgettable.

The next layer we examine is hypnotic language patterns. These are the ten persuasion patterns I have already given to you before. When you have these little micro-templates, known as persuasion patterns, you can literally insert or fill in the blank easy, with just about any type of command or suggestion you would like for your subject to carry forth or carry out it makes it so simple and easy to remember. If you haven't already committed to memory these ten persuasion patterns I recommend you stop reading at this time and revisit them and learn them. They are very important.

I mentioned as some point, also, that I'd be creating a flashcard deck which will be available for purchase on www.indirectknowledge.com at some future point. These cards will be laden with all types of very powerful, probably in fact some of the most powerful hypnotic persuasion patterns on the planet that you'll be able to pick up and purchase and memorize quickly and easily. Again, it is so easy—it's fill in the blank simple. For now though just go back and learn the ten I've given you in this book the best you can, so that as you go through your day you're actually beginning to consciously use them until which time they become very unconsciously used by you, and you use them just to be using them. The way language works is interesting. If you listen to a speaker, and you listen to him or her long enough, over and over and over again, you'll start to see patterns emerge more and more frequently. These are common expressions used by the most influential and persuasive people in the world. Your threshold of perception will increase as a result and you'll be critical of the language and specifically the words used by others to relay a point or communicate an idea.

The best preachers do this all the time. When preachers are pastoring over a church and they are giving sermons every Sunday and Wednesday you start to see these patterns become apparent. We become conditioned to the sermons. We become almost mesmerized to them, because of the consistency in certain patterns coming about.

The thing to remember is certain persuasion patterns are going to have a greater impact on your sermons over what others will. What we're doing with these patterns is we're actually expanding your range of ability in how you communicate certain suggestions and ideas—you're doing it very prolifically, so that the language you're using is intentionally helping drive home your points in the most powerful way possible. Most of these patterns have come from the modeling of the most successful preachers on the planet. I have learnt and dissected their linguistic structures and put them in such a way that you will be able to adopt them yourself for use in your own preaching. When you adopt them, you essentially get the same results—what you want! This is the whole idea behind this book. It's a model of what the most effective and successful preachers are doing so that you can emulate what they are doing and have the same exact results.

The next layer we can add is the ability to tell various types of stories. There are fables that are going to be very much geared towards on particular audience. There are English fairytales and folklore told to us as young children to teach us a moral lesson and instill certain values in us. We can infer certain things emotionally about these fairytales. What you want to do is when you're giving your sermons and telling these stories, you want to use stories that are appropriate for the context of the message you're delivering –and, certainly the various audiences you may be preaching to. You just need to be very aware of what these stories are going to do and the various impacts they will have on your listening audience. The types of stories you tell are very important, and you can use metaphors, similes, fables, narratives, talk about recent movies assuming it's appropriate to do so, different books you've read, stories other people have told you, stories from long past, or more recently relevant stories, and stories you make up even.

If I was going to tell a story, which my 82 year old father had told me about something that happened out of his childhood that would be considered relatively old and perhaps more interesting to someone nearer my father's age, or a young person who is curious about what children did for fun before the invention of the computer.

My father once told me this story about how as a child he would make his own bow and arrows from the branch of a maple tree and binder twine. What he said he did was take the binder twine, after whittling the wood clean, and attach it to the wood and then rub candlewax on the twine to make it tighter and more suitable for holding an arrow and tightening the line. He would make arrows out of cattail stems. I never would have imagined this, and the amount of creativity it took to come up with this is shear ingenuity in my opinion. A story like this could be used to discuss the differences in the evolution of creativity through generations. Today we talk of creativity as it applies to digital art and electric music. There were not around in Jesus's days on Earth.

There are a lot of things you can do with stories so please keep a timeline in mind in terms of your stories. Keep in mind there are various types of stories you can tell; whether it be metaphors you're using to assimilate certain ideas into your preaching message, or it's some type of narrative, having a lot of hidden meaning you want your audience to become aware of, the range of stories you can use is immense and worth investigating further outside the scope of this book.

The next layer is the ability to use extended quotes in our stories. We talked about this when we learnt about the Milton Model. These extend quotes are what we attribute to someone else as having said to us or somebody else. I could say, for example, something like: "My friend John was a boater and loved to boat. As a child his father was actually a fisherman. John literally grew up on a boat. John was telling me the other day in a very candid conversation we were having: "I was out on my boat. It was a beautiful day, very peaceful and serene. It was the most awesome weather there'd been in some time. The wind was blowing just enough to be perfectly pleasant. The sun's reflection on the water looked like shimmering diamonds; shimmering by the millions." John went on to tell me also, "It was very peaceful, and God had answered his prayer, as earlier in the week I prayed for such a day to happen." This would be an extended quote. It is not coming from me. I'm not actually telling it. I'm actually telling to someone else, i.e. my congregation, something that someone by the name of John, had told me. Because I can say this, it becomes more of a testimonial, backing up my message, in order to more convincingly share how good God is to those who pray. It can be stirring and motivational to hear such stories. It can bring home and illustrate certain things in the minds of your audience you want them to get which can be attributed to God's glory and majesty.

The next layer I want to cover with you are embedded commands. These are things I've mentioned a couple times by now throughout this book and I want to go into greater detail, now, with you on them, because they are the powerhouse of possibility that happens when you tell stories. These are really the secretive aspects of your story that your congregation is not going to be aware of. What many pastors do when they are delivering their sermons—especially these brilliant pastors who get the results they want and their churches become ultra-wealthy and successful at bringing more people to Christ Jesus—they use embedded commands in nearly every interaction they have with their sheep. This is something you want to pay attention to. So an embedded command is simply communicating on multiple levels. You're communicating one thing consciously to someone; however, unconsciously you're communicating something else to them.

You can think of it as though we have multiple brains in our heads—which we do—the reptilian, limbic, and cortex. These archetypal representations of the brain all have a different function. The reptilian brain is the instinctive brain. It is in charge of survival and reproduction. It is the part of the brain operating when we find ourselves in a tricky situation that catches us off guard—alone in a dark parking lot hearing unfamiliar noises that put us on high alert. We're certainly not thinking rationally, or even emotionally for that matter; rather, we're only concerned about our immediate survival and whether we should fight the unknown evils lurking to harm us, or flight away from them as quickly as we can hoping we don't get harmed. The next part of the brain is the limbic brain or what some refer to as the mammalian brain. This brain is developed from the time we're born to about five years of age. This brain is responsible for emotions. Some consider it the feminine brain, and look at its development from the point of view of a mother nursing her young in a very caring and nurturing manner. The love and emotions we're shown as a small child, by our mother and others, influences this brain, and when activated the limbic brain works to create meaning through feelings. As we go through our life this limbic brain is responsible for many of the decisions we'll make. One way to communicate with others is through emotions. People are able to intuit how we are feeling based on our physiology which is patterned off of our emotional states—for example, when someone is depressed they will usually reflect non-verbally someone who is depressed, meaning their shoulders will be hunched over, and they will be more reserved and have a sad or sullen expression on their face. We communicate all the time through the language of emotion through our behavior and body language. The last part of the brain is the cortex. This part of the brain is responsible for logic and reason. This means our ability to problem solve and strategize. Our emotions are not governed by this brain. This is purely our ability to rationalize an end result.

To summarize you have three brains each working like independent computers. One is responsible for survival instincts. When you hear a random loud noise and take cover instinctively without thinking, it is because of this brain kicking in and taking over. It is to keep you protected from dangers that threaten your survival. The next brain is the mammalian or limbic brain and is your emotional storehouse. It tells you how you feel, which, by the way, is often in conflict with logic and reason. This is why often times people will say one thing and do quite another. The last brain is the cortex which is the part of the brain that controls logic and reasoning functions. It tells us "how" to do something through thinking it through as a process. It sometimes gets rejected by the emotional brain, and we do things which are irrational. When people buy something they typically buy using their emotions, and later justify it with logic. This is why the best sales professionals will share an attribute of their product to prevent the instinctive part of the brain from outright rejecting it, and then give a logical reason for why it is important and useful, and then lastly give an emotional benefit of how it is going to make that person (i.e., new customer) feel after owning the product. We've talked about this in some detail when we covered the cognitive dissonance model of persuasion.

If you can think of the brain as having different functioning parts, and depending on what's going on in a person's reality, depends on what part of the brain is functioning. We can look at it almost as having two minds, and that's really the metaphor I'll use, throughout this book, that I've been using. I simply like to refer to it as the 'mind,' i.e. the conscious mind which we use to focus our attention on day in and day out, that is the things we need to be able to focus on and concentrate on in order to be able to get through our day. Then there is the 'other mind' which is the unconscious processes happening; namely, blood flow, heart pumping, breathing, and unconscious thought processes (e.g., dreams, self-talk, daydreaming, remembering a past event at random, insights, etc.). Some people call these two minds the conscious and subconscious but we're not really talking deepness, we're just talking two different minds; explicitly, one is a conscious mind, and one is an unconscious mind, but I just refer to them as the mind and other mind. I use these terms to identify the archetypal characteristics of the overall mind and how it functions.

So what we're doing is communicating on two levels. The way we do this is through analogue marking. If I say to you in a story: "My friend John was boating the other day and he had this thought enter his mind that he just felt and said to himself, 'You know John, you have to begin to *pray more often*,' and John was just thinking this, because he had prayed earlier in the week for a beautiful day, and this beautiful day came. Even when the weather man had predicted the weather would be miserable this day. John just new that praying made a difference and that God answers prayers." We'll stop here for minute and for brevity sake and make the point here, but the embedded command in that sentence "...pray more often," and we did that very indirectly through our character John, who happens to be a fictional character by the way, and we also told the story at the same time. So the conscious mind or 'mind' was just envisioning the story. The other mind was actually paying attention, though unconsciously, at the same time—it always pays attention. It was actually picking out the things I enunciated strongly, and you'll notice in the text here that I've actually italicized the embedded command in this sentence just to show a contrast and analogue mark the command.

If I were actually delivering a sermon I would have paused a couple seconds before I said 'pray more often' and then pause a couple seconds afterward. That's just enough time that the other mind can process that embedded command and begin to work on the psychological principles to persuade the listener to act on it.

To the listener this will seem like a random thought that strikes their conscious mind at some later point after the sermon, like maybe that night before they go to bed, and they will start to think that they too need to pray more often. It could be that, again, we attribute this to the other mind, or it could simply be the story's influence over the listener and how relatable it is for the listener. By relating, I mean people are listening to this story about how John doesn't pray so much, but when he did good things happened and he got what he wanted. Now they, the congregation, i.e. subject, may start to reason that if good things can happen for John when he prays, maybe they will likewise happen for them.

With embedded commands you can continue to deliver these embedded commands throughout your story and do so very indirectly and under the radar covertly, and they will start to germinate like seeds planted in the ground and they will grow into fulfilled actions, like a seed grows into a bountiful harvest. That's the power of a story being able to deliver these types of commands. Now, you can certainly use these same commands in your preaching, and very successful pastors I've modeled for the sake of producing this book, do exactly this; you'll hear them repeat the embedded command several times over and over.

To illustrate this point. On a televangelism program, towards the end of the program the preacher may say, "Listen to me. Listen to me. Listen to me," because he wants to focus his audience's attention directly on what he's about to say next, at that very moment where he's fixing to tell people to go to the phones and phone in a donation. He might reiterate certain effective adverbs by saying, "Quickly. Quickly. Quickly. Quickly. QUICKLY! Go to the phones! Quickly go to the phones. Quickly, quickly, quickly, go to the phone...go to the phone right now." He wants them to go to the phones, but he wants them to do so quickly.

This presupposes already that the individual will be going to the phones. Now he's bringing in a quality, which is "Quickly! Go to the phones!" By using this type of language it's creating an influence a persuasion over someone causing them to take action and quickly, without thinking about it, go to the phone. These embedded commands are very powerful. The best preachers and speaker in the world use them all the time; whether consciously aware of it or not.

You will have the advantage now of being consciously aware of it, and be able to *create these types of commands* on the fly as you tell your stories. Another thing I want to throw out, is another way to analogue mark your commands is to use a specific body movements to mark out your commands. This could be raising of your hand, and lowering of it once your command has been delivered. This will indicate to the other mind of your subject that this is important and in turn it will be resourced in the unconscious and acted upon accordingly. Another point to make on this is that this is very much in alignment and part of Pavlovian or respondent conditioning, which we've mentioned in our psychological persuasion models. People become conditioned at the unconscious level to act whenever a certain stimuli is presented, i.e. a raised hand. You'll see a lot of speakers gain compliance from their audience by asking for a show of hands, and raising their own hand, and watching the audience comply and do likewise. Good to keep in mind.

Our next layer, we look at, involve extended quotes. These are a must if you're going to be ultra-successful as a preacher. We discussed over these in some detail when we examined the Milton Model. These are quotes from other people that we speak of to elicit a testimonial perspective onto the audience. A lot of people in certain business fields will name drop extended quotes from noted celebrity-like authorities in the business community; namely, Warren Buffet, Peter Drucker, etc. They do this to elevate their own authority in business and to sell their idea to the audience as having come from someone with greater authority than themselves. People buy from those with greater celebrity-like authority than they do from those who have not yet achieved this status. If you're not already a celebrity authority in your field, i.e. a world class preacher well known around the world (e.g., a Billy Graham, Joel Osteen, Bishop T.D. Jakes, or a Dr. Mike Murdock, then you can attribute the ideas you want to convey as having come from them. If you ever watch any of these men preach, you'll see that they do exactly this when preaching their own messages to their audiences.

It was, in fact, the famed, Dr. Mike Murdock said to me the other day, "What you respect, you will attract," when sharing about an incident of when someone whom he greatly respected said to him, "Mike never permit greatness in your presence without celebrating it, recognizing it and acknowledging it in some way." Dr. Murdock was sharing that if someone of influence comes into your presence, celebrate them and reward them greatly; for they have done greatness for you in some large measure. This is a sign of deep respect.

Notice the above paragraph. I've made a point to you by using extended quotes to do so. I've named dropped Dr. Mike Murdock, founder of the Wisdom Center, and an incredibly influential and well known televangelist. I've also nested an extended quote by Dr. Mike Murdock, about someone else who had influence over him personally, developing an even more compelling persuasive argument. I'm telling you this is powerful, and it works. It works so well, that advertisers who create sales copy wouldn't dream of publishing something with-out first attributing what others had to say about a product into their message. Testimonials are a vital part of any sales letter. You may not believe me, but chances are you will more believe me when you believe other people, in fact a great majority of people, and even famous well-reputed people, believe me, and agree with me.

The next layer we'll add is the key dynamic of incorporating the artfully vague language patterns of the Milton Model, which we've already covered. These could be things like ambiguities (e.g., be aware, versus, beware). You want to incorporate some of these ambiguous language patterns into your sermons. The 'mind,' i.e. conscious mind can only process seven plus or minus two bits of in-formation at any given time; conversely, the 'other mind,' i.e. unconscious mind can process everything coming into it. Again, the conscious mind is the critical faculty or cortex brain, whereas the unconscious mind is the abstract creatithat ve 'big-picture' mind or limbic brain. When overloaded with information or hav-ing to exert too much mental energy to understand something confusing or am-biguous the subject turns off their reasoning and logic starts to go out the window. Whatever it is that you're saying then becomes accepted as though it's the Gospel truth. Use hypnotic storytelling in the most ethical conduct always, and never do harm with it; you'll probably, if you do, come to face some harsh punishment and the (d)evil will come back and knock on your door.

Next, we layer in sensory predicates. These are predicates that simply represent awareness. These words utilize the five senses; namely: visual, auditory, kinesthetic, olfactory, and gustatory. The reason you want to use a variety of these words, beyond the reason of cementing and really illuminating any story, is because many people process information dominantly through one of these five sensory systems. Most people are visual processors; formulating pictures in their mind, and making sense of these pictures by creating meaning. Others are primarily auditory in how they take in information. There are also people who are primarily kinesthetic, who lean on their emotions and feeling while processing through their sense of touch. The words you use that stimulate these responses builds far greater rapport with your subjects while also creating an easier go of assimilating mentally the stories you are telling them; viz., to help them become transported into your narrative much more easier.

An example, to illustrate this point, here's a quick story utilizing visual, auditory, and kinesthetic predicates:

> *I had just gotten home from a hard day's work. I had been toiling like a slave in an old black and white movie, pounding spikes so hard that even the occasional warning gunshots could only echo a pitch above the cold grey steel pounding against gold grey steel. I was tired, and all was silent when I entered my house, and without any lights on, and too exhausted to reach for the light switch the house was dimly lit; rather a perfect scene for retiring off to a heavy sleep watching such an old black and white movie. Ah the irony!*

This short story I just made up on the spot. I have incorporated the sensory predicates while also including the four parts of a stripped down hypnotic story; namely: (a) an event/routine (i.e., daily work) (b) interruption (i.e., home from work) (c) someone emotionally affected (i.e., main character), and (d) repurpose of an earlier element (i.e., black and white movie). The predicates are words like: hard (kinesthetic), old black and white (visual), pounding (kinesthetic), gunshot (auditory), echo (auditory), pitch (auditory), cold (kinesthetic), grey (visual), pounding (kinesthetic), silent (auditory), exhausted (kinesthetic), light (visual), dimly lit (visual), heavy (kinesthetic), and etc. This story primarily also uses an analogy to contrast work with slavery as represented in old black and white movies. Again, I made this up on the spot without any real effort, and the story is still a somewhat vivid and engaging story. Because the story is left without some detail (e.g., what type of work, etc.) it creates the Zeirgarnik effect; that is to say, leaving the audience left wondering what the missing details might have been. The audience will also create their own meaning to fill in the blank space to satisfy this need to live through the life of the character.

The other thing to mention is how some people have inner dialogues with themselves. In NLP we label this phenomenon of self-talk as 'digital dialogue.' All of these sensory predicates can be utilized to deliver a perceptive experience that inculcates the persuasive message more tightly into your subject's minds. Keep in mind that as you deliver your message that you don't want to go about delivering your message or story willy-nilly, because if you do, you'll have congregants who stop coming to your service. You want to deliver your story so people draw insights; namely, your hypnotic suggestions as being their own thoughts. People seldom want to do what others want them to do, but prefer to do what they want. Make your suggestions passively and indirectly theirs and you've mastered the art of persuasion. This is one reason you want to layer in sensory predicates.

Next we turn to syntax. We talk about passive language and direct language. Something can be spoken very directly—for example, "Get the mail." Or something can be said passively—for example, "The mail can be got anytime today, as you like." The first precedent is a direct command. Some people are turned off by being told what to do directly. People, after all, like choices or at least the illusion of choice. The latter precedent is a passive version of essentially the same sentence, though spoken in a submissive manner. Put like this, the command becomes more mentally acceptable, and therefore carried out without argument or the subject being critical.

There are times when you will be preaching a message and it will be proper, even more advantageous, to be very direct—for instance, at a time when you are reaching a crescendo –and, you really want to drive your message home. At this point you'll want to deliver some very direct commands and use a very direct form of language to best articulate your call to action. This will also charge the subjects and they will become excited and more and more on fire for God. Your ability to create these inner experiences using direct language commands will drastically help you influence abilities. It is interesting to watch people become instantly shocked, as if they just heard a gun fire off, when you become very direct with them. In NLP this is known as a pattern interrupt, and it is very useful for creating a shock value that drops them into an instant trance like state. At this point people will realize that this is serious what you're preaching, and it is imperative that they pay attention. You'll also want to include your emotionally laden language at these peak crescendos.

The crescendo is the climax of your sermon. Your sermon, if you want to think of it like this is really one long story. Inside this one story is various elements; namely, teaching, storytelling, explaining and giving Biblical wisdom, and many types of things which you'll incorporate throughout the whole sermon. So you want to keep in mind, when drafting and practicing your sermon your word order, i.e. syntax, and arrange your sentences strategically to create different affects you want to create in the minds of your subjects. Keep in mind that there are ways of being very aggressive and ways of being very passive and approachable.

This concludes the various elements you'll want to layer into your hypnotic stories. Again, you'll want to break each of your stories about 2/3rds of the way, depending on of course where your climax happens to be, to create the Zeirgarnik effect, and then start to tell the next story. You'll continue this process for five to twelve stories. This constant drop of one story is like a tease. You're going to tease your audience for the purpose of delivering your indirect commands so that they get picked up and processed by the emotional mind (limbic system) and not critically analyzed by the conscious mind (cortex). Indoctrination happens when this happens because the audience will act on their feelings which cannot be analyzed logically after the fact. Remember and don't forget that people buy and act impulsively through emotional processing; however, this doesn't mean people do not take action through logical and rational processing through their cortex brain. It just means that people tend to naturally make decisions without taking the time to weigh and consider all the pros and cons. If you are not following me here, please revert back to chapter 1 when we discussed the Chaiken case study—specifically, regarding heuristic and systematic persuasion theories.

Another point to make mention of is that when people are decision making and acting at the unconscious emotional level they are not thinking linearly so much, and are in fact learning at the unconscious level. We talked about the four types of learning and how when someone learns something to the point it be-comes unconscious and natural for them to carry out something without thought to it, they don't necessarily know why they know what they know, or fully know what it is they know, but they exhibit the behavior of someone who has mastered the subject material. This is exactly what starts to happen when someone carries out your indirect suggestions, believing that the suggestions or what they con-sider ideas, are actually their own insights. You can learn something consciously and eventually get to the point where it becomes an unconscious response. When you're telling these stories your subject's will go to the place where they simply start to act compliantly. It is the same thing that happens with a post-hypnotic suggestion that a hypnotist delivers to a subject—thus why these stories are hyp-notic stories. People begin to act. They don't know why they're acting. They just start to do things, because it just feels right to them, or sounds right, or looks right to them. These are things that have all been done through conditioning. You've actually, over time, sermon after sermon, conditioned your congregation to be warriors for Christ and to have a Christ-like concern for all people, and to share the Gospel with others, and do so in such a profound way because in a sense they are doing it so unconscious. They are unconscious of the fact that they're doing what they need to be doing according to the Bible. It makes it very easy for them to do, without having to second-guess themselves, or God, or enter into long religious debates that do not produce the desired end results that Christ has called upon us to put forth and bring about. It becomes a very easy process; help-ing the ministry to grow, the income of the ministry to grow, and so that God's message can be spread throughout the world.

What If You Apply Hypnotic Storytelling Differently?

Let's think about what if, for a moment. Let's think about going beyond simply hypnotic storytelling with the method I've laid out for you. What if we change things up a little bit? What if we modify some things? This is what's called exper-imentation –and, it's perfectly fine to utilize or discover new ways to use hypnotic storytelling in ways that are going to influence and persuade your audience. For example, you could, instead of one long nested loop in your storytelling, in other words where you tell one story; break it 2/3rds of the way through, tell another story; break it 2/3rds of the way through, tell another story; break it 2/3rds of the way through, and continue that process until you start to complete the loop and circle back around to the first story; rather, you could have nested loops nested inside of nested loops. What I mean by this, and again this is going to take a high level of skill to do well, and your ability to remember each story told will need to be on point, this is something which definitely will have to be thought out in advance most likely, or something you'll over time acquire the skills necessary to act on successfully. You could begin telling one nested loop variation and after telling 4 or 5 stories you could on your fifth story complete that loop and then go back to story 4 and complete that loop, and then not complete story 3, and instead begin telling a new story; story 6. You could tell the seventh story and the eighth story, and then after making your breaks in those stories (as many stories as you want to go) then you can start to circle back around yet again and when you get to story five you'll simply bypass it as you've already completed that story, you'll bypass story four because you've already told this story as well. Instead, you'll swing up to story number three and finish this story, and story number two finish this story, and then story number one, your first story, you'll complete this story as well. See what happens. See what affect this has on your audience. The more dynamic your stories are, the more persuasive, the better for your ministry.

Telling stories in the way I've just suggested, as an example, could be something that could really not so much confuse your audience necessarily, but really keep their minds so focused on what you're doing and saying, letting them process your persuasions mentally and emotionally, while one part of them consciously remains somewhere else. You could start to play with your audience in how you direct their attention and focus to discover what happens.

I've heard it relayed by many other trainers:

"Energy flows where attention goes; attention goes where energy flows"

—*Anonymous.*

I've heard analogies give illustration to this, as well. One is the phenomenon many of us can relate to, where you're driving along and you're going in one direction and then then your attention gets taken off guard by something random or out of place (e.g., a raccoon runs sideways to where you're going) so you start to go into a completely different direction, automatically following towards the raccoon you've been eyeing. You take the car with you, or it could be that you're riding a bicycle and take it with you, in the direction of the small animal you've become fascinated by and which has taken your attention away from the course you were charting.

I was once riding my bicycle down a relatively straight path, and at some point I noticed a steep ditch, and very soon found myself in that ditch. The ditch became a pattern interrupt that took my attention away from what I was focused on and sent it somewhere altogether unplanned and in my case undesired.

These stories and as you're directing attention and focusing it elsewhere, where you want to focus it, these are things you can also keep in mind. That you're telling a narrative which is you're taking people down a story, down a timeline, down a space, and there's energy happening and matter being formed in the mind, some of these images will be generalized, some distorted, and other pictures will be deleted as if they weren't even said by you the storyteller. The main thing to keep in mind is you're in the driver's seat and wherever you want to lead other people they're essentially looking to you. If you happen to veer off course they'll naturally veer off course, because, again, their focus and attention is on you and what you're telling them.

So keep in mind as you're going throughout this book, and you're learning these lessons that I'm giving you on persuasion and influence; keep in mind that this book is the not Gospel in anyway, obviously, and that you are free and in fact encouraged to test and try some of the various psychological persuasion models I've presented you with, try some of the hypnotic language patterns found in the Milton Model, try some of the meta model violation patterns you've discovered learning the Meta Model, and to try out some of the cookie-cutter, fill-in-the-blank, preaching persuasion patterns I've given you as well. Try them out! See what happens. See what happens when you layer them into your stories. Discover new ways to do things, which make you an even more prolific storyteller. Discover learning from an educator's perspective to where you're actually being an innovator and creating and discovering new models, frameworks, and blueprints that define you as a storyteller and person of influence and master persuader. This is what researchers and theorists do; we go through and we analyze, hypothesize, experiment, test, and discover correlations about cause effect situations, that can be modified to certain contexts—determining what works best to bring about the most effective end results we seek.

When we discover something as being more beneficial or advantageous than something else we've been using, then that is what we start to work with instead. We do more testing, analysis, measurement, until we have a near-perfect model to share with others. You're very much encouraged to do the exact same thing.

Many of the best preachers in America and around the world whom I have modeled their language, behavior, beliefs and attitudes, whom shall remain anonymous, are in fact doing exactly this. They are constantly testing their persuasive messages. Much like a marketing department for a company will do the same. Where marketers will A/B split test two different commercials, modified slightly, relatively the same message, to determine which commercial is the most effective for creating more sales; these top of the line preachers will do the same thing. They will learn a sermon by memory and throughout the course of preaching it over and over again they will test various subtle changes to determine the results achieved. Is the offering-plate heavier with money? Are more people coming to Christ with sermon *A*. v. sermon *B*.? They continue to do this over and over and over again, and it's no wonder, if you think about it logically, why so many pastors end up memorizing their sermons; continuing to regurgitate the same message over and over again, to multiple audiences. Once they discover one sermon is so developed and powerfully persuasive that it has a guaranteed affect effect on just about any audience, they will, in fact, look for other outlets to share this persuasive message—building a name for themselves. This of course has a compounding effect; meaning, the more well-known a pastor becomes the more influential and persuasive he becomes. We observe this happening not only in Christianity, but also with Indian gurus who have gained international notoriety and following, and many other such religious groups, and other key players in the world of personal development and other fields. What essentially happens is these pastors achieve, besides a cult-like following of sheep, but they also achieve celebrity-authority status amongst preachers—dominating the world of professional preaching. Being innovators puts these preacher's names on the map. God blesses these great persuaders, because of their due diligence, education, and willingness to go above and beyond by constantly honing their skills.

If you've been called to the ministry to preach I highly recommend you do the same; that is, you learn to mirror, mimic, and model these great teachers and preachers, because they certainly will not be around forever to do the work of God. New preachers will need, in my opinion, to come into the fold and be able to continue on the work of God which has come before them. These new preachers will need to take what has been discovered and start to evolve preaching for the greatest good of humanity. I think personally, that's what's needed.

If you happen to be a new pastor preaching then these are things to keep in mind. Don't settle for mediocrity. Don't settle for average. You're here to do a job. God has called you into his preaching ministry to do something and do it to the best of your ability. It is God after all that we're talking about here.

Don't play games with preaching. Don't play games with the ministry. Do the very best you can. Apply what you can that works, until which time it has been proven in your mind and results to be effective almost 100% of the time, if not 100% of the time. If you can achieve this, you'll start to help people in ways unimaginable—all for the glory of God.

The Monomyth

The Monomyth is also referred to as the Hero's Journey. The Monomyth is a thread that runs through nearly every single myth and epic throughout history. It is the quintessential story. Hollywood and Bollywood screenwriters have used this framework as a guide to produce some of the bestselling, most popular, movies to ever hit the box office.

Joseph Campbell can be attributed with discovering this common thread that runs through nearly every mythological story. Campbell, lived an uncommon existence, teaching mythology, learning himself about a range of subjects from religion, philosophy, anthropology, and many more. He hated being confined to a narrow restricted education. Campbell, relating the intentions of the Hero's Journey, described it as a self-discovery, rather than a courageous act.

"Greek and Latin and biblical literature used to be part of everyone's education. Now, when these were dropped, a whole tradition of Occidental mythological information was lost. It

used to be that these stories were in the minds of people. When the story is in your mind, then you see its relevance to something happening in your own life."—Joseph Campbell

Why the Monomyth?

I want to share with you why you need to understand the Hero's Journey or Monomyth so you can use it to tell more intriguing stories. Why you need to learn the structure of the Monomyth is because it is found in nearly every great mythological story throughout history—at least some aspects of the Monomyth.

We can for example look at the biblical account of Moses. We know about his early childhood, being raised in the Pharaoh's household, though by birth he was a Hebrew (Israelite). Eventually, as a young adult, Moses kills an Egyptian who was beating one of his own. Moses is then forced to Midian where he lives a practically normal existence for nearly forty years or so. At some point he's called by God to enter the "Hero's Journey" or "Monomyth" which is when he starts to take instruction from the burning bush, and go and through a series of events along this journey bring his people out of bondage and delivers them to the Promise Land or Land of Milk and Honey. This whole process is structured as Campbell's Monomyth—it's a powerfully influential and persuasive story about how having faith in God can free you from limitation and deliver you to better place that is more rewarding and valued.

We see this Monomyth example in so many different stories, and in so many different fables, and in so many different narratives and screenplays and so on and so forth. It is important, because it's a story that takes us from normalcy and routine and everyday existence to identifying with following after some pursuit to achieve some end-result; namely, some boon, favor, advantage, or benefit. It could also be some knowledge or wisdom which we seek or some treasure.

I remember reading Paulo Coelho's fable titled: The Alchemist. I read this book many times, first when I was a small child. This fable, if you've read it, is yet another example of the Monomyth. There is a young shepherd boy, living out a very boring existence day-to-day, who surrender's this existence to go in search for a great treasure. The journey begins, and the young man learns many things along the way, and experiences a sort of metamorphosis. It was a very prolific fable and one that I would have to say is one of my favorites. Its life changing, like so many other well written books are—like for instance, the Bible.

The Monomyth is this identification that everybody can relate with and have had, where we have dreams or some aspiration or thought of grass being greener on the other side or there being a destination, dharma, or as we call it in Christianity, a calling. This calling is fundamentally a call to action for us to do something and possibly achieve some result through blindly stepping forward and chancing everything will work out given that God is guiding us along this journey. For many people this journey is a choice they refuse to take a step in the direction toward, for whatever reason. In this case the dreams remains a dream. For others the journey is the chance to enter a new reality and escape the everyday norm. It can after all be an exciting proposition to step out into the unknown and trust God to provide and see us through. The pros out weight the cons and for these people the journey begins and takes place. There are rewards for taking the journey. There are rewards for traveling to places unknown and foreign. There's an education that happens only through such an experience. There's new and exciting happenings taking place, yet also bad and dangerous consequences as well. There's right and wrong choices. There's opportunity to turn back, or keep moving forward. There's the constant mental anguish and regret from time to time. In the end, after the result has been achieved, there's the hesitation of returning back to the old way of being and living, or remaining in the new world as you are.

So the Monomyth is a story people can easily relate to and identify with inside themselves. In many ways this type of story is incredibly inspiring and even altering in a sense to an audience member; that is, your subject. This is why it is important to understand what the Monomyth is so you can utilize during delivery of your sermons when appropriate.

Joseph Campbell when he was alive came up with seventeen steps that comprise the entire Monomyth. Many of these steps are not present in every mythological narrative; however, many of them are seen. We'll now take this journey together in theory and learn about the Monomyth, so you can achieve better results with your storytelling by utilizing the model I'll be sharing with you. This will let you frame such stories quickly and easily and get you to the point where you will be able to influence and persuade your subjects in a new profound way and to other audiences.

The last reason you should really learn this Hero's Journey; that is, this Mono-myth, is because so many Hollywood screenwriters utilize this exact model for developing their own works which have frequently become Hollywood block-busters. These stories have brought in many millions of dollars in revenues for such Hollywood films. This is proof enough for me that the Hero's Journey is one that brings about results and can be trusted to do the same for you.

What Is The Monomyth?

I think mentally as we consider what every great myth or story has which has been well received by audiences is a central character. This character begins with having lived an ordinary existence—one, for the most part, lived since birth. The character grows up in a particular society adopting a defined culture with certain norms and expectations regarding how life should be lived. It could be an Indian child who grows up having a father owning a small shop, whose father before him owned that same shop, and so on for many generations. The expectation has been since birth the son would take over the family business carrying on the tra-dition. It's expected.

In any example we might pull, from any culture which can be pulled from, we'll find examples of how different people believe life should be lived. There are many of them, and many differences exist amongst these cultures. Differently, these cultures adopt the societal beliefs, religions, norms, expectations, consider-ations, and so on.

I think when we stop and contemplate the common thread running through each of these cultural stories we begin with this idea of normalcy from the van-tage point of the culture observing itself. There is a regular routine for a charac-ter living in such a culture. It could become for the character a symbol of identity, boredom, hierarchy in society, status, value, and a map for living life. The char-acter self-identifies with this culture. He or She knows the ins and outs from con-ditioning since birth or becoming indoctrinated into the culture at some earlier point. It is a real challenge for the character to sometimes see past what is; rather, more comfortable to simply accept one's lot in life and not look to greener pas-tures.

Somehow through some means the character learns or gains insights about another culture, a foreign land, or peoples, or religion. This difference is the contrast that starts a shift in the story. There's a buildup of desire which causes tension to occur within the character, until which time there is no other option mentally for the character except to embark on the journey to the new land.

The discovery of the foreign land, people, new language, new religion, has an affect over the character—a strong hold. The character starts to wonder what it would be like to live and exist in that culture. What it would be like to embrace those beliefs. These may be very subtle thoughts. They may be very direct. They could be brought on simply due to their difference and contrast from the culture the character exists within. One thing is for sure this new world is outside the norm or reality for the character and somehow that's appealing to him or her on some level.

Through some possibility or some account or happening the character is given an opportunity to pursue the journey over to the new world. Though there's typically barriers one must face, as not everyone is worthy to enter the new world. There's usually some guardian at the gate or price to pay to experience the new world. We relate to this in our modern day age with having to have a special visa to enter several foreign lands. Without a visa, entry is forbidden. It is the same thing with the character in a myth. There's usually this barrier to entry that makes it difficult, yet all the more sought-after, because people want what they can't typically have. There's an attraction to gaining what you are told you can't have. It's a challenge. It's very much psychological.

The character becomes confronted with a choice. Is entry into the new land worth the price of admission? The character starts to weigh the pros and cons to decide once and for all will I stay or will I go. Deciding to stay in ones' own world can be deemed as patriotic and nationalistic whereas leaving can be termed an adventurer a person brave enough to pursue their dreams and aspirations. The critical mind of the character can spin words to define their own actions and live in peace with whatever decision they choose to make.

For the most part, in most novels, I might guess every novel or myth, the character decides to take a leap of faith and go for it. They suspend their disbelief about what they rationally know about the new world, and make it a sort of imaginary world in their minds. They then dart off in the direction of the new world, and take the Hero's Journey.

It's not certain what the outcome of the story will be. In the beginning of every story there is no certainty—only a sense of adventure. How far the character makes it into the journey is uncertain. There's so much uncertainty.

The common thread observed by Campbell was that often times these characters will undergo some type of initiation. This is an induction into the new world. This is the entry point I discussed that leads to the decision to embark or disembark the journey.

At some point; maybe sooner rather than later, or later rather than sooner, the character finds a mentor or a mentor finds them. This is a coach. A wise figure that gives guidance and wise counsel in which the main character is not yet aware of. Eventually the character crosses over the threshold into the new world. The character starts to come to terms with the quest or mission and certainly the new world itself. The journey begins, and imperceptibly changes start to happen inside the psyche of the character as the narrative unfolds. These changes are slow and steady building on one another strengthening the character. A metamorphosis happens that transforms the character into a hero from having been an ordinary nobody. Leadership happens. The character comes face to face with weaknesses and is forced to utilize his or her resources to conquer problems that crop up along the journey. These problems are character tests to force the turtle out of his or her shell making them to confront life head-on. It's David facing Goliath in the moment with nowhere to run and hide.

If the character is willing and able to overcome such trials and tribulations the character experiences some intrinsic reward and self-confidence and starts to believe in him or herself. These test teach us what the character is made of and give us (the audience) a different understanding of our underdog. We can't help except to side with the character and cheer him or her on.

The character doesn't give up; rather, keeps pursuing the journey. There is, after all, an assignment, a pursuit, that keeps the character focused and traipsing forward.

Another common thread that runs through many of these myths is love, or some spiritual realization or experience with divinity. Usually this is some person, an entity, a thought, realization, or God experience, which has significance and higher consciousness. This phenomenal experience gives meaning and purpose to the mission, augmenting the necessity to complete the mission. Sometimes this experience is an internal awakening inside the character forced out by strong thoughts in a weak moment. This is usually the point in the narrative where the character becomes emotionally seduced by the mission. It is often times at this junction where the greatest impact in the story happens.

Then there are temptation that are found in many of the myths. These temptations lead to the possibility of adjournment of the journey. Maybe it becomes an easy way out altogether; stopping the quest completely. More often we observe a temporary setback and not an abrupt end, however.

Later there's atonement. This could be with a character possessing great power. We often observe a father or father-like figure—for example, it could be a situation where in the past the character has had a conflicting disagreement with the father figure, and now at this point the relationship gets repaired. Most often we see a positive effect from this atonement, and usually a repaired relationship.

Apostasis happens afterward in which some character, likely the fatherly figure, dies either a physical death or dies a sort of mental death to take on living a more divine-like existence; possibly embracing love, supreme knowledge, or some higher understanding of life. This is a death to their self, to perhaps live in divine knowledge or love, or to become more compassionate and blissful. They put away a side or aspect of themselves which is no longer working for their existence.

The main character ultimately realizes the mission and receives a boon for accomplishing the journey. This is usually the end result the character had in mind. This is what the character has went in search for of found as a result of taking the road less traveled, so to speak.

At some point another decision much be made. The character earlier, toward the beginning of the story was faced with the challenge of deciding whether to attempt to cross the threshold into the new world or not. Now, the character must decide to remain in the new world or exit it returning to the old world.

Sometimes the case is the character doesn't wish to return home to their ordinary boring existence. The mission is over and the character has grown after all in strength and character. Now it is time to return or not. If the character doesn't return, we take it to mean they don't want to return to the normality they once were accustomed to living and embracing. They have at this juncture become quite far removed from the old life, adopting a new life, that returning becomes just as difficult as was leaving in the first place. It is impossible in some cases in part from the transformations which have occurred for the character to return, and so they don't.

Usually, around this time, a flight happens, because some drastic evil has entered the picture to regain back the object won-over by the character. At this point the character must protect what has been gained and retreat to a safer place. Sometime this induces a great rescue to come about in the story, i.e. another character, a secondary character, may have to rescue the primary character. Sometimes the character becomes weakened as a result of a fight with some evil character, and this other secondary character comes along to ensure the primary character is able to retreat safely back to some other location.

The threshold of return is when the character decides to go back home from whence he or she came. This means taking with them the newfound skills and abilities and incorporating these new aspects of themselves back into their old environment and lifestyle. Integrating these learnings learnt from the journey into ordinary life again happens.

Then there's mastery. Mastery is where the character starts to balance between the physical and spiritual world. It is crucial to note that spiritual may be the memory of the journey or even the lessons learned of a higher nature or calling. These lessons have helped them return back to their life, only changed dramatically as a result.

This is essentially the Hero's Journey. This is what you can begin framing some of your stories around. Essentially this is a framework for change and eliciting the thoughts that subtly surface as the story reveals itself. It is a very hypnotic journey, and a form, but not format that must be adhered to strictly.

I love stories, if you can't tell. Stories make us forget who we are and help us discover who we want to become. Stories are representations of life in many ways. They teach us much better than facts and figures tell us. They allow us to become involved emotionally, making us to feel part of something outside of ordinary. Ordinary is for the critical thinking mind; that is, the mind that functions consciously through the cortex brain or what some might call the male brain. The Hypnotic Hero's Journey is the other mind, the subconscious mind or unconscious mind, what some refer to as the female brain that is the limbic system. In many cultures it is the mother who reads us bedtime stories and inspires our imagination, let's us play make-believe and pretend, encourages us to consider other people's emotions and feelings, and teaches us about abstract thoughts like good and bad. The mother nourishes our amusement and wonderment and helps us to make life more than what it seems it is.

The father is rational and logical and strict. We apply the principles of right and wrong to outward actions. The father teaches us to think critically, not be blinded by our emotions, and to forgo what he labels impracticality—most of what the mother has taught us to embrace with our heart and inner self. These polarities are found in stories we read and watch on the big screen. They represent the battle of the minds; that is, the mind and the other mind, constantly in conflict. Regret is when we do something from the heart and later realize it was an irrational mistake. Regret is also when we do something logically only to wonder what might have been had we pursued it from the heart, i.e. other mind, and not the critical mind. Really understand that this is the rudimentary key to all persuasion and therein lies the key to indirect and direct hypnosis approaches, which we use as tools to influence people into making the changes we want them to make. Some might call this manipulation while others may call it helping someone get to a better place. It all depends on the context. It is the same with any tool. A doctor can use a knife to save a patient's life, while a murderer can use a knife to kill someone. Again...be ethical and well trained in how you use the persuasion and influence tools. They can help people, but they can also hurt people. Always do good work. Never do evil.

How to Apply the Monomyth?

The Monomyth is a design structure that can be used as a blueprint for telling and sharing stories with others. This structure has been argued by some critics to be constraining. I have not personally found this to be the case. In my mind, having some structure is like having the wise guide that we encounter in the Monomyth just before we cross the first threshold into the new journey. It is the hand-holder and inspiration coach that motivates and persuades us almost without persuading us. The structure is there for us as a guide, but not as a rule or in my opinion even a rule-of-thumb. It is simply there to help us tell a great story should we decide to consult it for advice, when we get stuck. In my opinion such a literary device is actually useful for inspiring creativity and lessening the fatigue and stress of fighting or waiting for a burst of insight and inspiration to strike down upon us. Knowing it's there for me takes the pressure off allowing me to tell a less restricted story and one that is more intuitive and one in which I keep my audience in mind more expertly.

Let's now learn about the profundity and richness of each part of the Hero's Journey, i.e. The Monomyth, and talk about how to implement it into your sermons.

I.   Character begins in normality; that is to say, a normal, relatable environment. This stage is important for setting the stage, because it depicts a contrast with what's to come. When you're starting your sermon story, you'll want to discuss how people live their lives based around their environment. The environment is one of conditioning. We resist change, and therefore we hesitate when opportunity presents itself. When God calls us to an assignment we often times mentally rebel.

II.   Character undergoes an initiation in which they're introduced and inducted into a whole new world. The opportunity sounds enticing; that is, like a chance to depart the boredom and entrapment of ordinariness. It also causes the critical mind to begin to weigh the pros and cons of taking the new assignment. During this process the character begins to take an assessment of what will be lost taking the assignment, while unsure of what will be gained. Anything new often times seems enticing, but it also presents with it a sense of uncertainty and unsureness which causes many people to think twice about taking the assignment.

III.   Character gets a mentor who serves as a wise guide. This guide has wisdom and insights the character doesn't. The guide is almost like a salesman who reassures the character what is involved in taking the assignment. When you're preaching and delivering this type of story you'll want to make mention of the types of attributes such a wise guide has. When Moses led the Hebrew peoples out of Egypt and into the Promised Land, he served as a wise guide in a sense. There was insecurity in making such a drastic change, but Moses kept reiterating how God had in store a plan for His people. The attributes of Moses may be one type of archetypal representation you'll want to paint a picture of.

IV.   The character is confronted with the first threshold; to be precise, this threshold is a barrier to entry into the new world. This could be a test of character and strength that must happen. This threshold is guarded by other characters who protect the new world from those unworthy of entry. When God is on our side, who can be against us? This is a point that will inspire your subjects to ask questions about whether they are truly called to take an assignment or if they are simply wishfully thinking that God has called them. It is an important point to emphasize, as those truly called will be faced with obstacles that must be overcome in order to follow the path laid for them by God. This is a test of faith most usually.

V.   The character must come to terms with the new world upon taking the first step of the journey into the new world. One we decide to move forward and have committed we often second guess if we should turn back. We contemplate whether we have made a mistake or not taking on the journey. There must be a mental strength of endurance and a certainty that builds in the mind which causes the character to be absolutely resolute in proceeding with the mission. Once we've embarked upon the journey there's no turning back. Often times accepting the journey and crossing over the first threshold brings with it the impossibility of turning back to the old life. This happens when the character goes against the advice and ultimatums of the people and culture of his or her past. It is sort of like saying, "If you go, you are not welcome back. So you better be absolutely sure of your decision."

VI.   The character faces trials along the journey. These are tests of his or her ability to survive and problem solve the journey. Nothing is given us or handed to us without some character building and testing. These tests and trials create changes in the character and personality of the person. This is along the lines of the cliché, "What doesn't kill us it makes us stronger." There's usually a subtle series of changes that take place creating a metamorphosis within the character. Those we know from the past would not recognize us as a result, but the character is usually unaware of the changes taking place within him or her.

VII.   The character endures some type of supernatural experience in which a god-like love or experience happens to alter the beliefs and mindset of the character. This could be the Burning Bush experience Moses experienced. This type of experience brings greater clarity and an invincible belief within the character letting him or her know that they must continue on in the journey and that their journey is not without purpose. This is usually a highly motivational experience that builds an internal strength in the mind of the character.

VIII.   The character comes into temptations that causes them to rethink the journey in lieu of stepping off the path to take advantage of some material gain or secondary opportunity. Jesus was tempted by the Devil; namely, offered the world if he would pledge His allegiance to him. Jesus declined. In some stories the characters may temporarily step off course by the illusion of temptations.

IX.   The character makes atonement with a power possessing character. This is usually a fatherly figure or someone from their past who has great influence over them. When confronting the ultimate power figure who has held power and control over the character the character makes peace with the character alleviating a great harbored pain and weakness that has held them back mentally. This is usually the center point of the story. When you're preaching you'll want to make a mental note of this being the center of the story. After this event occurs the protagonist is in control of himself or herself and regrets he or she might have harbored from the power figure are let go of. Many times when people are brought into the Christian fold they face criticism and discouragement from the power figures in their lives. A teenager may face retribution from an antagonist parent figure trying to dissuade them from their decision to trust and follow and have faith in Christ Jesus.

X.   Some character in the story undergoes Apostasis; namely, when they die a physical death or death to the self in which they realize some higher purpose or transition to another realm, i.e. heaven. This could be a mentor who dies or someone who has contributed faithfully to the protagonist's mission. In your preaching you can bring out examples of the people who stood by Christ and Christianity throughout history who became martyrs for the cause of sharing the good news with others.

XI.   An ultimate boon is received; that is, the purpose of why the protagonist has taken the journey is fulfilled. The realized goal brings a sense of accomplishment. This is the Promise Land realized, essentially for the Egyptian peoples.

XII.   Many times we see the hero protagonist unwilling to return back home to where their life was ordinary. They have changed. The change has become their new reality. The idea of going back to where they began seems like a distant past that no longer resonates or defines who they are. They are now a stranger to this past and it is uncomfortable and unthinkable to return back to that reality. It would be like the fishermen disciples after following Christ Jesus not wanting to return to the ordinary life of fishermen. Instead it seems more probable they would want to become leaders in the new church and spreading of Christ's teachings.

XIII. After receiving the boon the protagonist is often faced with antagonists rivaling to take the boon away from him or her. In such cases the protagonist must escape with the boon.

XIV. The main protagonist is often times injured at the point of achieving his or her mission. In this event the main character must sometimes be rescued by some guide or secondary character. This character could act to serve them and nurse them back to health and wellness for a period of time.

XV. There comes a time when the protagonist must become confronted with the return threshold. This is the point in the story where the protagonist begins to realize the wisdom gained from the quest, and starts to integrate this wisdom back into daily life, and possibly they will share this wisdom with the rest of the world or their inner circle. This is the lessons we draw from a story. The Bible for example is a book filled with valuable wisdom drawn from characters which has been written down and which is now shared around the world with those accepting the faith. Stories themselves are emblematic of human experience and life.

XVI. The protagonist must learn to balance the inner world and outer worlds; viz., be emotionally and critically sound in decision making and moving his or her life forward. We cannot live from a place of logic and reason always, because emotions and intuition play a part in the psyche of the subject. We're teaching through our preaching the principles of maintain a healthy and balanced existence—we must take the assignments we intuit and feel God has given to us, while at the same time being conscious and able to live from a place of reason and logic in order to critically think our way through problems and obstacles that will continue to land along our life path.

XVII.   A journey of such magnitude and which has altered our thinking and beliefs about what we're capable of means we are no longer afraid or fearful of death as we have mastered life by undergoing the uncertainty of the journey we've treaded. We are now a master in our own right and able to guide and teach others in the way of following the heart and head to their own assignments given them by God. Your preaching can reflect this teaching and mentoring to your congregation (i.e., subjects). Again, keep in mind, a story is a representational picture of life. A story can teach us and influence us in many ways to follow the path God has presented us with.

We have covered the Hero's Journey or what is called the Monomyth. The journey is empowering and communicates to the subject on many levels. The story inspires, motivates, encourages, guides, leads, and captivates the attention of your audience. Storytelling bridges the divide between the mind and other mind; namely, the male (critical faculty) and female (affective/sentimental) brains. A story or narrative transports the subject to places of wonderment and enchantment giving them an experience they cannot know in ordinary normal life.

What if We Use the Monomyth As a Model?

It is important, I feel, to not be stifled in your storytelling. A model should not suppress your creativity and ability to tell stories. Some may argue that such a form is actually a formula. It isn't. The form of this Monomyth structure is only the principle thread running through most myths and narratives. It is a form to make your storytelling easier. It is the same principle which applies to the hypnotic persuasion patterns I've presented you with in chapter 2. You can take away what is useful while leaving what isn't behind for another story.

Knowledge is power. You are not restricted except by ignorance. It would be equal to the experience of having never read your Bible and trying to share the Word of God with others. You may be able to, but the journey would be less pleasant and likely more painful for you. Having a form to serve as your guide, is like having a general knowledge of the Bible without having to memorize the entire Bible in Its entirety. You'd be able to more easily point non-believers in the right direction having a general overview than you would otherwise. Having a hypnotic persuasion pattern which you can use as a cookie-cutter template when the need arises to persuade someone to take an action is arguably better than memorizing an entire persuasive sermon verbatim as much as it is better than giving a sermon without any study or idea of what to talk about or present.

All of this being said do not get bogged down by rules and formulas. There are no hard rules to storytelling, only wise guides. Love runs deep in stories, and 90% of storytelling is the love and emotion behind the words; meaning, 10% is the structure used to convey your persuasions. When the mind and other mind are in conflict the other mind will always win. Emotion always is more persuasive than logic and reason. Emotions are at the heart of forgiveness. Even when someone messes up and makes a poor decision it is emotion that often lands them forgiveness by the jury. Emotions are addictive and transferable and cause tears to shed and without reason. Emotions are not something you can logically explain away. This is why LOVE will always magnetize people to Christ Jesus, injecting in their hearts a shot of emotional elixir that creates permanent change and a Christ-like concern for all people.

You see I can explain all of these persuasion models with the greatest logical arguments; just like I can tell you a story begins with normalcy and ends with a great emotional resolve that depicts a life-changing moment. Remember, stories are a reflection of human existence. People only know what they know and when it comes to emotions we know what they are in one sense; yet, we know them better through how we feel; however, we cannot explain them logically. What does it profit a man if he gains the world but loses his soul? Emotions are the soul, the world is the logical argument.

I should mention, before we dip our toes into the deep waters of Jesus's Parables, you should want by now to turn off your critical mind, and turn on your emotional mind. It is time to speak in a way that others feel our meaning even though they cannot logically or linguistically explain it absolutely. The language of emotion, in my opinion, is the Language of God. We observe this in the Parables of Jesus.

The Hypnotic Parables of Jesus

A parable is a didactic narrative that expresses and edifies a universal truth; it is a simple narrative. It is both indirect and direct. It is indirect in the way it is told, yet paradoxically its meaning is not intentionally covered up; rather, directly meant to be understood. A parable is short, and different from a fable in that its direct object is humankind, and not animal or something intangible.

In the Bible Jesus' parables are a perfect story. I love parables. Parable sketch a setting and this setting becomes etched in the mind of the subject. Parables have an action and they have a result. I could tell you a parable, but Christ Jesus already has, and so I share Matthew 13: 1 – 53 with you.

I want you to read the parables in this section of the Bible; rather than tell you a parable myself. Keep in mind how 90% of a story is the emotional affect and only 10% is the logical form itself. Try not to cry for no reason. I find myself often unable to keep a dry eye. I have gotten so many insights from this passage. I cannot articulate them for you; they must be experienced. I urge you to really suspend your disbelief or critical thinking and let your other mind take reign—you know the mind where miracles are possible and pretend is allowed to co-exist with logic and reason. Without the former the latter is dull and lifeless in my opinion.

> *King James Version (KJV) Matthew 13: 1 - 53*
>
> *The same day went Jesus out of the house, and sat by the sea side.*
>
> *¹And great multitudes were gathered together unto him, so that he went into a ship, and sat; and the whole multitude stood on the shore.*
>
> *³ And he spake many things unto them in parables, saying, Behold, a sower went forth to sow;*
>
> *⁴ And when he sowed, some seeds fell by the way side, and the fowls came and devoured them up:*

⁵ *Some fell upon stony places, where they had not much earth: and forthwith they sprung up, because they had no deepness of earth:*

⁶ *And when the sun was up, they were scorched; and because they had no root, they withered away.*

⁷ *And some fell among thorns; and the thorns sprung up, and choked them:*

⁸ *But other fell into good ground, and brought forth fruit, some an hundredfold, some sixtyfold, some thirtyfold.*

⁹ *Who hath ears to hear, let him hear.*

¹⁰ *And the disciples came, and said unto him, Why speakest thou unto them in parables?*

¹¹ *He answered and said unto them, Because it is given unto you to know the mysteries of the kingdom of heaven, but to them it is not given.*

¹² *For whosoever hath, to him shall be given, and he shall have more abundance: but whosoever hath not, from him shall be taken away even that he hath.*

¹³ *Therefore speak I to them in parables: because they seeing see not; and hearing they hear not, neither do they understand.*

¹⁴ *And in them is fulfilled the prophecy of Esaias, which saith, By hearing ye shall hear, and shall not understand; and seeing ye shall see, and shall not perceive:*

¹⁵ *For this people's heart is waxed gross, and their ears are dull of hearing, and their eyes they have closed; lest at any time they should see with their eyes and hear with their ears, and should understand with their heart, and should be converted, and I should heal them.*

¹⁶ *But blessed are your eyes, for they see: and your ears, for they hear.*

¹⁷ *For verily I say unto you, That many prophets and righteous men have desired to see those things which ye see, and have not seen them; and to hear those things which ye hear, and have not heard them.*

¹⁸ *Hear ye therefore the parable of the sower.*

¹⁹ *When any one heareth the word of the kingdom, and understandeth it not, then cometh the wicked one, and catcheth away that which was sown in his heart. This is he which received seed by the way side.*

²⁰ *But he that received the seed into stony places, the same is he that heareth the word, and anon with joy receiveth it;*

²¹ *Yet hath he not root in himself, but dureth for a while: for when tribulation or persecution ariseth because of the word, by and by he is offended.*

22 He also that received seed among the thorns is he that heareth the word; and the care of this world, and the deceitfulness of riches, choke the word, and he becometh unfruitful.

23 But he that received seed into the good ground is he that heareth the word, and understandeth it; which also beareth fruit, and bringeth forth, some an hundredfold, some sixty, some thirty.

24 Another parable put he forth unto them, saying, The kingdom of heaven is likened unto a man which sowed good seed in his field:

25 But while men slept, his enemy came and sowed tares among the wheat, and went his way.

26 But when the blade was sprung up, and brought forth fruit, then appeared the tares also.

27 So the servants of the householder came and said unto him, Sir, didst not thou sow good seed in thy field? from whence then hath it tares?

28 He said unto them, An enemy hath done this. The servants said unto him, Wilt thou then that we go and gather them up?

29 But he said, Nay; lest while ye gather up the tares, ye root up also the wheat with them.

30 Let both grow together until the harvest: and in the time of harvest I will say to the reapers, Gather ye together first the tares, and bind them in bundles to burn them: but gather the wheat into my barn.

31 Another parable put he forth unto them, saying, The kingdom of heaven is like to a grain of mustard seed, which a man took, and sowed in his field:

32 Which indeed is the least of all seeds: but when it is grown, it is the greatest among herbs, and becometh a tree, so that the birds of the air come and lodge in the branches thereof.

33 Another parable spake he unto them; The kingdom of heaven is like unto leaven, which a woman took, and hid in three measures of meal, till the whole was leavened.

34 All these things spake Jesus unto the multitude in parables; and without a parable spake he not unto them:

35 That it might be fulfilled which was spoken by the prophet, saying, I will open my mouth in parables; I will utter things which have been kept secret from the foundation of the world.

36 Then Jesus sent the multitude away, and went into the house: and his disciples came unto him, saying, Declare unto us the parable of the tares of the field.

37 He answered and said unto them, He that soweth the good seed is the Son of man;

38 The field is the world; the good seed are the children of the kingdom; but the tares are the children of the wicked one;

³⁹ *The enemy that sowed them is the devil; the harvest is the end of the world; and the reapers are the angels.*

⁴⁰ *As therefore the tares are gathered and burned in the fire; so shall it be in the end of this world.*

⁴¹ *The Son of man shall send forth his angels, and they shall gather out of his kingdom all things that offend, and them which do iniquity;*

⁴² *And shall cast them into a furnace of fire: there shall be wailing and gnashing of teeth.*

⁴³ *Then shall the righteous shine forth as the sun in the kingdom of their Father. Who hath ears to hear, let him hear.*

⁴⁴ *Again, the kingdom of heaven is like unto treasure hid in a field; the which when a man hath found, he hideth, and for joy thereof goeth and selleth all that he hath, and buyeth that field.*

⁴⁵ *Again, the kingdom of heaven is like unto a merchant man, seeking goodly pearls:*

⁴⁶ *Who, when he had found one pearl of great price, went and sold all that he had, and bought it.*

⁴⁷ *Again, the kingdom of heaven is like unto a net, that was cast into the sea, and gathered of every kind:*

⁴⁸ *Which, when it was full, they drew to shore, and sat down, and gathered the good into vessels, but cast the bad away.*

⁴⁹ *So shall it be at the end of the world: the angels shall come forth, and sever the wicked from among the just,*

⁵⁰ *And shall cast them into the furnace of fire: there shall be wailing and gnashing of teeth.*

⁵¹ *Jesus saith unto them, Have ye understood all these things? They say unto him, Yea, Lord.*

⁵² *Then said he unto them, Therefore every scribe which is instructed unto the kingdom of heaven is like unto a man that is an householder, which bringeth forth out of his treasure things new and old.*

⁵³ *And it came to pass, that when Jesus had finished these parables, he departed thence.*

Chapter Summary

In this chapter we covered simple storytelling structure, hypnotic storytelling structure, the Monomyth form, and the hypnotic parables of Jesus. We learned how emotions are embedded in stories and how stories can be a reflection of human experiences.

Stories typically convey a message that can be direct or indirectly conveyed in a story. They can be intentionally indistinct or not deliberately distinct.

The storytelling models presented are there to use as a guide; however, the real power of a story comes in how the storyteller puts into words the message's emotional undertones. Expressing emotions linguistically is an art rather than a replicated formula. Everybody is different and this uniqueness will make distinct your stories from everybody else's stories.

When I was a child I used to ask my father if he liked this song and that song, and his reply: "I am not taken by the song, because there's no heart in the singing." He would tell me about this singer and that singer from when he was a child, he heard, who had heart; lamenting how music today is mostly commercially produced without the passion and feelings behind the music.

Think about this for a moment: a simple, imperfectly sung church hymn can have someone in the congregation weeping tears of love for Jesus, and why? The answer is the love and passion behind the music. This is the power of telling a story. Even an imperfectly told story will have greater affect than a perfectly told story if you'll tell it with sincerity, emotion, and heart—like you would if you were singing a beautiful hymn for Christ on a beautiful Sunday morning. There's something unexplainable that makes you feel good and walkaway feeling truly blessed and grateful for all that you have and for the people in your life. Tell your stories as you might sing one of these songs and you'll brilliantly get your message across to the extent that if affect the crowd and though they will not be able to articulate how they feel with words they will be influenced and touched by the story. Everything you do; do with kindness and love for others.

Action Steps

The following actions steps are meant to help you bridge the great divide from theory to action. I've heard it said that 80% of self-help books never get read all the way through, and only 20% of people ever complete the action steps found at the end of each chapter. Maybe you've heard of the 80/20 rule:

"So the 80/20 Principle states that there in an inbuilt imbalance between causes and results, inputs and outputs, and effort and reward."

—*Richard Koch*

In other words, 80% of the wealth winds up in the hands of 20% of the population. Twenty percent of products contribute to eighty percent of sales. This statistical discovery has been labeled Pareto's Law, after its founder, Italian economist, Vilfredo Pareto. Pareto in 1906 discovered that 80% of Italy's land was owned by 20% of the population. Significantly, this is found in economics, business, and many other disciplines to ring true; where 20% of some group will benefit from the efforts of the other 80% of the population of that group. These imbalances create leveraged opportunities for those willing to capitalize and do what the 20% does, while avoiding what the 80% doesn't do. I'm sure you can relate this back to one of our persuasion models if you go looking for it.

Suffice to say, I want you to be in the 20% of action takers and gain the true value of what I have to teach you. Certainly the choice is yours, and I'm not there to strike the back of your hands with a rule-stick; however, should you decide to pursue the true value, you'll gain the most, and realize the rewards that 80% percent of the readers won't. Not everyone will be truly great—will you?

I will be repeating this exact same intro to the action steps for each chapter. Do not be alarmed and think I'm doing it on accident to fill up pages. If I wanted to fill up pages, I'd increase the font size and double-space the lines, and add in a bunch of filler; I wouldn't do that to you! Remember back and recall the first words of chapter 1:

"Only what we keep hearing do we believe."

—Bryan Westra

I.   Make yourself tell multiple stories keeping in mind the principles taught in this chapter. Practice until your stories become an unconscious extension of your everyday communications.

II.   Watch for people's reactions to your stories; specifically, keep an eye out for facial expressions and body language. The subject's reaction is valuable feedback to you about your performance. Look for softening of facial muscles and rapid eye movement and dilated pupils—these are indicators your stories have achieved a hypnotic affect.

III.   Embed the earlier learned hypnotic persuasion patterns into your stories. Press upon your subjects positive suggestions that will help them fulfill the work of Christ Jesus. Keep your stories sensitive so they elicit emotional reactions from your subjects. Remember that emotions are contagious and what you feel others will feel as well. Tell your stories using congruent emotions that parallel the messages of your stories. Practice always and continue to hone your skills and perfect your art.

CHAPTER 4

How to Build a Persuasive Sermon that Moves People & Maybe Mountains

In this chapter we'll talk briefly about how to build a persuasive sermon that sells your message. We'll begin by discussing Monroe's Motivational Sequence; a persuasive structure developed by Alan Monroe at Purdue University during the mid-1930s. Then we'll look at how to architect a sermon from beginning to end incorporating elements of what you've learned in previous chapters.

Keep in mind it is not within the scope of this book to teach you how to form sermons of every type. You are hence encouraged to learn about other methods of sermon development from other resources. What this book will provide you with is a powerful method of sermon development that is geared for regular church services. If you are to give a sermon at a funeral or perform a wedding you'll want to study from other resources exactly how you might accomplish this. This book is designed for the purpose of delivering persuasive sermons and preaching for camp meeting and televangelist type sermons and similar contexts.

I want you to stop for just a moment and reflect on this journey we've taken thus far. You've learnt a lot, and might consider how much more you know over many other preachers delivering regular sermons. Take a moment to digest all of this, because at this interval in the book we're transitioning over to delivery applications. Everything that has come before this point has been to serve you as a resource for applying the individual aspects; namely: the psychological persuasion models, linguistic styles, and storytelling blueprints to enhance the skills you already possess. This chapter is meant to give you a framework for sermon creation to prepare you for delivery.

Monroe's Motivational Sequence

Monroe's motivational sequence is what's taught in many public speaking courses at university when students learn how to deliver persuasive speeches. Many sales courses utilize this structure as well. The sequence is a series of five steps. Each step is logically ordered to create a persuasive effect. Follow the steps and you'll have the keys that open the door to persuasive speaking and presenting.

Many of the best preachers utilize this very sequence and with great success. You're encouraged to do the same. The sooner you master this five step sequence of delivery, the sooner you'll be unconsciously delivering speeches, sermons, workshops, lectures, and other forms of public speaking without having to give much thought to the steps necessary to deliver a persuasive presentation.

This single tool is one that you'll use over and over again with great success. It will also help you to lift the blanket of staleness in your church and encourage your subjects to get on fire for carrying out Christ Jesus' teaching—helping them to take actions that promote God's instructions for them.

Why Learn Monroe's Motivational Sequence?

Learning Monroe's Motivational Sequence will provide you with something easy to recall. It is also psychologically persuasive as well as psychologically motivational. Motivational and Personal Power coaches often employ this sequence when delivering their motivational talks and seminars. It has been shown to be highly effective.

I have personally used this sequence while delivering product presentations in my previous career as a sales professional—bottom line Monroe's Motivational Sequence works. I have taught this very sequence to college students and sales professionals and the feedback I've gained from both groups has been positive. Students share with me how easy they find it to be when implementing and giving a speech. Sales professionals tell me how it helps them sell more. I've never heard any negative feedback come to think about it.

What Is Monroe's Motivational Sequence?

Monroe's Motivational Sequence consists of the following sequences: (a) attention, (b) need, (c) satisfaction, (d) visualization, and (e) action. This sequence starts with attention; a common start for many persuasion, hypnosis, NLP, sales, marketing, and advertising models. In marketing for example there is the AIDA model: (a) attention, (b) interest, (c) desire, and (d) action. Notice how in this common copy writing framework it begins with attention and ends with action. Many models utilize these and similar elements. However, let's turn our attention now to how we can use Monroe's Motivational Sequence.

How to Use Monroe's Motivational Sequence?

Let's take Monroe's Motivational Sequence one sequence at a time and discuss each. This way we can gain more insight into each of the five steps. This will also give you greater clarity and perspective on how you might want to utilize it to form your sermons. With Monroe's Motivational Sequence the structure is important, because each step leads into the next. You'll want to complete each step before moving onto the next.

I. **Attention:** The purpose of attention is to overcome apathy from the listener (i.e., your subject) by redirecting focus in a way that elicits excitement, goodwill, and respect. To apply this first step you'll want to turn to your creative faculties. You can for instance use startling statements, questions, illustrations, anecdotes, background material, or reference to the subject or occasion of what it is you'll be talking about. In public speaking where you'll be delivering a persuasive speech you want to throw something out that will instantly in the first couple seconds grab the subject and capture their attention—so be creative. Keep in mind people have short attention spans and if you don't grab their attention with something impactful, it could be that you lose them; namely, leading to boredom about what it is you're talking about, causing your message to get lost to noise and the self-talk clutter happening in their mind.

II.   **Need:** The purpose of need is to describe the problem in such a way to make it personal to the subject. Whenever there is a need there is an opportunity for a solution—a need is a problem. Problems create pain, and it is from this painfulness that you'll architect your message to make it personal to affect the listener. You'll be eliciting an emotional response. How you achieve this sequence is by creating a statement of need in which you point out what's wrong with the situation or problem. You may want to embellish how bad the situation is and explain how if the problem persists what is likely to happen as a result. You'll also illustrate the high-points of the problem by citing specific incidents which helps to make the problem more important. This is when the subject starts to associate the problem and lessen the dissociation in which they have perceived the problem at a distance. This creates the effect in which the subject begins to realize that now is the time to confront the problem/pain. You'll talk about the ramifications in which you cite the facts surrounding the problem. This could be where you present example, quotations, and short parables, to make the argument more persuasive and impressive. Lastly, you'll want to relate the problem back onto the audience showing the relevance and how the problem will affect them personally.

III.   **Satisfaction:** The purpose of satisfaction is to present your solution; namely, in a way your subject will make sense and feel as though it is actionable. You'll want to present the solution is the form of a request. Indirect hypnotic persuasion patterns can be useful here. Every problem has a solution. Solutions bring pleasure; while problems bring pain. People's tendencies are to avoid pain/problem while embracing solutions/answers/pleasure. This is a psychological principle of persuasion. How you can go about implementing a satisfaction strategy is by presenting your proposed action in a way that is clear and concise; easily understood by your audience. Make sure you're actions are timely, attainable, and realistic. You want to be able to paint a picture in the mind of your subject in which the process is being undertaken, like a mind-time-line. Make a logical argument for why the action(s) will work and why it's the best course of action to take.

IV.   **Visualization:** The purpose of visualization is to future pace your subject into the future at a time when they can visualize the problem being resolved or left unresolved. This is the place in your persuasive talk where you'll intensify desire through this visualization process. You can utilize awareness words like: let's say...., imagine..., picture it..., what will happen when..., how do you think...., and so on. How you can apply this step into your persuasive speech/sermon is by having your subject's see the problem resolved if the solution/action(s) you're proposing are carried out. You can also take the negative and paint a picture of what will likely be the situation if your solution/action(s) are not carried out. Monroe also teaches that we can adopt a mixed approach showing both sides of the coin.

V.   **Action:** The purpose of action is to make a call to action that a response is needed from your audience. A powerful impact will be made during this sequence. You'll end on a strong emotional note invoking an emotional response from your subjects. How you'll achieve all this is by challenging or appealing to your subjects by having them left feeling or believing a certain way while you make a specific appeal to them to take a precise action. You'll also summarize your main points and in the process advocate the exact beliefs and actions the subjects should adopt that are aligned with your desired outcomes. You can utilize persuasion patterns and emotionally laden language during this action step. You can also include a powerful quote, illustrative story, or a personal statement of intention letting it be known of how strongly you feel about adopting the course of action you're advocating. When you present an illustration you can also present an example of when a similar solution was used to solve a similar problem to help make your case.

Here's an example of all the actions utilized to help make this motivational sequence more explained:

Listen to me! God has given me a message especially for you today! God knows how life throws you curve balls. You've been working and not getting ahead for a long time now. There's a solution though. God's solution. All that is required is trust and faith in Christ Jesus. Imagine a few weeks from now how much you will have grown in Christ when you are reading your Bible and a sudden burst of insight and emotion strikes you somewhere deep. A place you've never been. A journey not yet taken. If you don't start having faith and trust in God, or start reading your Bible regularly, the penalties will be that you'll follow the path of resistance, and you'll continue feeling as though you'll never get ahead, ever. Can you help me by reading your Bible each night, praying private prayers seeking God's love? I feel strongly that God has given me this message and that if followed out it will grow our church and improve how we help others. Church immerse yourself in that love, and build trust and faith to the extent that you know things are changing—altering us in a considerable respect! Can you help me? I implore you to learn from your Bible each night—the Word of God is infallible. This is what's needed and required by God, now.

In the above example, though short, all the sequences are covered in order. Even so, this example has a lot of room for improvement. A better attention grabber can be implemented. In the example I used a lot of vague language patterns in which there is very little content. I could have used a quote, example, or something more to make the case for action. There should be more emotionally laden language used. At best, this example shows how possible it is to apply all five sequences in a short period of time. You'd of course want to expand and add in more persuasion patterns and be more specific about what it is you wanted.

What if You Adopt Monroe's Motivational Sequence?

You can expect when you apply Monroe's Motivational Sequence that your sermons and preaching begins to take on a newfound potency. You'll be more convincing sounding and able to articulate your point of view and counsels in a way that will be much more compelling as well as actionable. People will want to follow you to the four corners of the Earth to ensure that your suggestions are taken and acted upon and carried out to completion.

The more you practice applying this model the more capable you'll become at instantly and effortlessly—even unconsciously—using the five sequences to make a convincing presentation. This means you'll start to persuade your subjects to follow you almost blindly as you chart the course and give the instructions as to the direction your church is headed. This puts you in a very powerful and almost enigmatic position as a leader; especially, when you consider the difference between you and most other average preachers; those who don't know or know how to use the artfully vague language patterns of Milton H. Erickson, and many other persuasion patterns and models you have learnt owning this book.

The Complete Sermon

Now the fun part. We're where we've been wanting to get to since we embarked upon this journey of learning about influence and persuasion principles and models; namely, to learn how to architect the most persuasive and complete sermons possible that will have the great impact on your audience. First and foremost you begin with the audience in mind. There is a common mistake made by newbie preachers, which is to write a sermon based around their own likes and dislikes. Any type of writing requires knowing your audience and writing for them and not necessarily for you. So get focused on your sheep and not yourself.

This structure of the complete sermon begins with a skeleton that is Monroe's Motivational Sequence. After the skeleton is put together the next step is to start fleshing in the skeleton with the persuasion techniques you've learned in this book.

Every church requires donations (tithes) from its people in order to keep the lights on and do the work of Christ. The sermon we will construct as an example is one to encourage parishioners to pay their tithes. If you a new preacher nervous about asking for money from your worshippers then this will help you—by all means use this very sermon if you like, customizing it to your unique style.

Why Deliver the Complete Sermon?

You want to adopt the practice of always delivering the complete sermon; meaning, you want to present the strongest argument possible without lessening or leaving out anything in your message. You have to be careful, however, because you don't want to be one of those longwinded preachers who loves the sound of their own voice; unable to recognize your audience doesn't.

The complete sermon must be conveyed to have the greatest impact on your congregation. In sales they have a saying, "You're only as good as your last sale!" I want to borrow this and apply it to your preaching:

"In preaching you're only as good as your last sermon!"—Bryan Westra

Simply put, this means you're remembered week to week, service to service, by your previously delivered sermon. If people start to become bored they will start to focus their attention elsewhere and this could mean finding another church to attend—with a less boring preacher—not to mention a unified congregation of likeminded and excited aspirants ready to claim a leadership position under such a great leader like yourself.

So this is why you must always deliver the complete sermon; never taking shortcuts in your preparation or your delivery. Be sharp. Be well organized. Be emotionally congruent with your message. Make every word count.

What is the Complete Sermon?

A complete sermon is one where you can walk out to the lectern and begin, deliver, and end your sermon in a timely fashion with the greatest impact on your audience. It is a sermon that misses nothing; yet, seems perfectly presented. It is a sermon where your congregation is steadfast listening, fully engaged, and afraid that if they do not give you their full attention that they might miss out on something of tremendous value to them. It is a sermon that affect everyone in the building and transcends ordinary. It is a sermon that outdoes every other sermon heard before.

The value found in delivering a complete sermon is the difference between a full offering plate and a pitiful one. You can, as you know full well, attribute a small offering to externalities or internalities. You'll recall chapter one when you learned the attribution model of persuasion. If we're receiving small offerings it can be attributed almost always to the impact you message has had persuasively on your subjects. You have to sell your message in a way that is convincing enough to force your subjects to want to give and feel as though they have no choice but to give to God what is God's.

Many people unconsciously donate money directly proportional to the amount of value they receive. In other words, donating is paying what you think you should pay, given the quality of the sermon received, and how the subject walks away feeling. Elsewise, cognitive dissonance can occur, causing the attendee to feel bad having given more than they thought they ought to. In one sense, as preachers, we're entertainers, teachers, advocates, sales professionals, master communicators, and able to keep someone from paying the price of eternity in Hell. The value preachers provide is invaluable. Still, to be truly successful you owe it to yourself to deliver the highest quality sermon and most complete sermon possible.

How to Compose the Complete Sermon?

This is where the "rubber-meets-the-road" as they say in sales. We'll begin with Monroe's Motivated Sequence, and then start incorporating everything we've learned up to now.

Remember, our sermon is on why our subjects should tithe ten percent of their income.

To help your church grow here's my recommendation and what I'll do for you: (a) make this a mini-sermon, (b) deliver this the first Sunday of each new month, (c) append this onto the back-end of a high quality substantive sermon you'll deliver first, (d) ensure you deliver this sermon before collecting your offering. I'll create this sermon for you; that is, I'll structure it out, and make it a sort of mini-sermon that you can practice with and perfect month after month throughout your preaching career.

The reason you want to deliver this sermon the first Sunday of each new month is because many people receive government checks around the first part of the month. Delivering it the first Sunday, after they have received their checks ensures that the funds are there for them to give. If you were to deliver it at the end of the month chances are the money will have been spent. This way you help your subjects pay their tithes without the money burning a hole in their pocket. This also helps ensure that Church bills are paid on time and gives you opportunities throughout the rest of the month to ask for necessary funds and offerings as well.

First things first before we construct the sermon. We need to do some preliminary research. This means tying action to the Word of God. This is very important, because people want and should be doing what is advocated in the Bible. Since the Bible is the Word of God, i.e. God, it is deductive to think that if the Bible says do it, you should do it. Following God's instructions is not optional, and therefore your subject's should be made to follow those instructions. This is important to always keep in mind. If you find yourself letting your subjects believe they have a choice you're not doing your job; rather, you're being influenced and persuaded by your congregation, and essentially causing them to sin against God. You are the chosen leader and if you're ever not leading; rather following, then you need to seriously do some praying about your calling. Seriously!

There are many great resources today to help you quickly and easily find in the Bible exactly what you're looking for—even without knowing the Bible so well. Don't worry some of the most effectively persuasive preachers do not have the Bible memorized or even quite so many verses memorized. They do however have certain key verses memorized. After you deliver this mini-sermon month after month you'll have the money-producing verses likely memorized and rolling off your tongue.

One of the first resources, besides the Bible and flipping through its pages, are some software resources which you can feely find and us online. Some paid resources are also worth exploring. One of the more popular ones for preachers, and which helps you plot and plan your sermons with a built in word processor program is E-Sword (http://www.e-sword.net/). One of my other favorite re-sources is http://biblehub.com. This online resources has a built in concordances (e.g., Strongs, etc.), as well as sermons to reference, and the site makes it easy to find any topic in the Bible with easy and quickness. You can search around for other resources as well to find the ones that work best for you. These I've men-tioned happen to be my favorites. I also recommend these resources as they'll give you the ability to reference many different Bible versions. Many churches and Christian sects prefer the original King James Version, and these resources give you that option as well as many others.

For this mini-sermon on tithing I've visited http://biblehub.com and typed in 'tithe' and found the verses needed and which I've used in this sermon. If you want to visit this site and do the same you can see exactly the verses to see how I reference them in this complete mini-sermon.

Sermon Title: Jacob's Dream

Attention
Quote Technique:

Voltaire once said, "When it is a question of money, everybody is of the same religion."

Need
Relevance Technique:

I have to ask you: What is sadder: a church that cannot pay its bills or a Christian who pays lip service, and doesn't tithe? Are we the same religion as any other which Voltaire would argue we are? Do you obey God's instructions or merely pretend to be different and believe that God is the most important aspect of your existence?

This is important church. This is important.

People make excuses that are external excuses. They say, "I don't have the money to give; given I have this bill to pay, and that bill to pay, and I'm not rich, or if I pay my tithe, I'll suffer for it." I say to you, "God has given you everything you have; you, in fact, have everything in because God has blessed you with it. Paying your tithe is your recognition of this fact. Paying your tithe is a decision that is inside you; not outside you. Because you pay your tithe, God blesses you more and more. The more you recognize the power of paying your tithe, the more God blesses you. Church. Church. Church. Pay attention to this. Paying your tithe should be automatic and done cheerfully, all the days of your life. You can't excuse your behavior by attributing your lack of giving to some external cause; for it's the internal recognition you will pay your tithe that has you paying it, and being blessed for doing so. Have faith in God. Have faith in God church.s

Everybody—every one of you here today is *fortunate* to be here—pay extremely close attention to what I'm going to give you—it is a precious, precious gift; the same gift God gave Jacob in a dream—a gift of prosperity!

God has a message for you; a message that is never easy for any preacher to deliver, yet one that God requires me to present to you and give you instruction in.

You must pay tithe; that is, one tenth of what you are blessed with. If you are blessed with ten dollars; you must give one dollar to God. If you are blessed with $100 dollars; *you must give* $10. If you are blessed with $1000 dollars; *you must give* $100 dollars. If you are blessed with $10,000 dollars; you must, listen to me now, *you must give* $1000.

Hear me: It is not a gift you must give; you must give a tithe, i.e. a tenth back to God. God does not give you the option; rather, God gives you the instruction. God gives the gift to you; however, God instructs you must give a tenth to the Church. It's not my instructions—it's God's Word that instructs you to do so.

In you Bible, your instruction manual, God conveys how this tenth or this tithe is holy unto the Lord. In Leviticus 27: 32 we read:

"And concerning the tithe of the herd, or of the flock, even *of whatsoever passeth under the rod, the tenth shall be holy unto the* LORD.*"*

In Numbers 18: 20 – 32 God is clear in his instructions that a tenth; that is, a tithe is given to the work of the tabernacle. This tenth is commanded to be the best part of what you are gifted with. This tenth is given over to the work of God. God instructs you to give a tithe; that is, ten percent of everything you are blessed with that it is allocated to doing the work of the Lord.

You may be thinking what happens if I don't deliver my tithe? You might be arrogant enough to think that you deserve all of what is given you by God, yes? People do, I'm sure, and I've seen it by their unwillingness to comply with God's instruction to pay a tithe.

In Malachi 3: 8 – 10 God asks some questions, doesn't he? You want to know what those are, don't you? I'll tell you, because it's my job to tell you. God has commissioned me to tell you this, and I must obey the Word of God; as everyone in God's house here today must obey the instructions of God.

Everyone point to your neighbor and say, "You must obey the instructions of God" (Observe that everyone complies).

"Will a man rob God? Yet ye have robbed me. But ye say, Wherein have we robbed thee? In tithes and offerings. Ye are *cursed with a curse: for ye have robbed me,* Even *this whole nation. Bring ye all the tithes into the storehouse, That there may be meat in mine house, And prove me now herewith, saith the* LORD *of hosts, If I will not open you the windows of heaven, And* -*pour you out a blessing, that* there shall *not* be room *enough* to receive it.*"*

This is a problem for many people. Robbing God is a serious offence; especially, given that everything you have, EVERYTHING, you have because God has blessed you with it. Everything! I don't own anything that God hasn't given me! Everything I own God has blessed me with! Everything!

Satisfaction

Proposed Action Technique:

I want to recall for you a story. It is the story of Jacob, which we find in the 28th Chapter of Genesis. Open your Bibles with me to Genesis 28, verse 10 (Observe Compliance from Subjects).

Jacob's Ladder

"And Jacob went out from Beersheba, and went toward Haran. And he lighted upon a certain place, and tarried there all night, because the sun was set; and he took of the stones of that place, and put them for his pillows, and lay down in that place to sleep. And he dreamed, and behold a ladder set up on the earth, and the top of it reached to heaven: and behold the angels of God ascending and descending on it. And, behold, the LORD stood above it, and said, I am the LORD God of Abraham thy father, and the God of Isaac: the land whereon thou liest, to thee will I give it, and to thy seed; And thy seed shall be as the dust of the earth, and thou shalt spread abroad to the west, and to the east, and to the north, and to the south: and in thee and in thy seed shall all the families of the earth be blessed. And, behold, I am with thee, and will keep thee in all places whither thou goest, and will bring thee again into this land; for I will not leave thee, until I have done that which I have spoken to thee of. And Jacob awaked out of his sleep, and he said, Surely the LORD is in this place; and I knew it not. And he was afraid, and said, How dreadful is this place! this is none other but the house of God, and this is the gate of heaven."

The Stone of Bethel

"And Jacob rose up early in the morning, and took the stone that he had put for his pillows, and set it up for a pillar, and poured oil upon the top of it. And he called the name of that place Bethel: but the name of that city was called Luz at the first. And Jacob vowed a vow, saying, If God will be with me, and will keep me in this way that I go, and will give me bread to eat, and raiment to put on, So that I come again to my father's house in peace; then shall the LORD be my God: And this stone, which I have set for a pillar, shall be God's house: and of all that thou shalt give me I will surely give the tenth unto thee."

Church! The Lord is in this place. Turn to your neighbor and exclaim joyfully: The Lord is in this place (observe compliance).

Jacob understood and even vowed a vow to give the tenth of everything unto God. A vow is something sacred, is it not? A vow is a promise we keep. Keeping our vows is a reflection of a Christ like character.

The problem with many people is they don't take their vows serious enough. Church this is serious business. It's God's business.

The solution is simple, church; we'll honor our vows and pay our tithes—we'll be different, and pay our tithes. Our church will pay our tithes; a tenth of what God gives us to the work of the Lord. We'll not steal from God.

Paying to God what is God's means we'll always have a growing Church; meaning, we'll ALWAYS be ministering to the lost. God will continue to bless us for it. We'll ALWAYS pay our tithes.

Turn to your neighbor and tell them, "We'll ALWAYS pay our tithe so we will ALWAYS grow as a church" (observe compliance).

Visualization

Forward Thinking Technique:

Let me paint a picture for you. Imagine, if everyone in this building, everyone here who professes to be blessed by God, pays their tithe, i.e. their tenth of every blessing they receive.

What would happen to our Church?

Think about it. (Long intentional pause)

Month after month. Year after year. Think about it.

> *The point is this: the one who sows sparingly will also reap sparingly, and the one who sows bountifully will also reap bountifully. Each of you must give as you have made up your mind, not reluctantly or under compulsion, for God loves a cheerful giver. (NRSV) 2 Corinthians 9: 6-7*

Our Church will grow. More people will come to Christ Jesus and hence to our Church. Our Church will be blessed for your willingness to give God what is God's. You must have this vision in your heart. You must know your reason for coming here. God has called you here not to take; rather to give. We give God our commitment by waking up early on a Sunday, like today, and committing to sing hymns of praise. Committing to learn the Word of God. Committing to prayer. Committing to sharing our testimonials which prove God's blessings in our lives. Committing to paying our tithe, because we believe in doing so with a cheerful heart. Committing to growing this Church as outlined in our Christian Bible.

Think about how many people will be in this building next year. The year after that. The year after that. The year after that. Impressive, isn't it? This is the power of multiplication; that is, the power of God's blessing us through honoring our vows. We will honor our vows.

Turn to your neighbor and say, "I will honor my vows."

Think about how different this building will look and how when new people enter these doors they will be amazed to find how much God has blessed his people. This will happen, because we will pay our tithes.

Turn to your neighbor and say, "This will happen because I will pay my tithes."

Action
Summary & Appeal Technique:

I could be wrong, but I don't think Voltaire was talking about our Church. I don't think that we are like every other religion. I believe, and you have shown me today, that you are all cheerful givers. You are cheerful of the blessings you have received from our Lord and Savior Christ Jesus. You have all committed to paying tithes—acting like Jacob who woke up early one morning, vowing a vow, saying, "If God will be with me, and will keep me in this way that I go, and will give me bread to eat, and raiment to put on, So that I come again to my father's house in peace; then shall the LORD be my God," and vowing a promise: "all that thou shalt give me I will surely give the tenth unto thee."

I could be wrong, but: Imagine this. Here you are; you all are present in your Father's house this morning. You have all vowed a vow here today. Imagine this. Here you are; like Jacob was in the Old Testament, vowing a vow that has stood the test of time. Imagine this. Here you will be when years have passed and your vow has blessed not only this church; but rather, has blessed you beyond measure unimaginable.

Repeat this vow after me: "If God will be with me, and will keep me in this way that I go, and will give me bread to eat, and raiment to put on, So that I come again to my father's house in peace; then shall the LORD be my God."

Finish this promise vow by repeating after me: "all that thou shalt give me I will surely give the tenth unto thee."

Imagine what this promise, first made my Jacob, has led to. Imagine how blessed we are today because of Jacob's promise to God. Now imagine how blessed we will be a year from now because we are still keeping this promise to our Lord and Savior Christ Jesus. It's a promise I'm happy and cheerful to keep.

Let's keep our promise Church. Let's pay our tithe, because God loves a cheerful giver. (Pass the offering).

Sermon Notes

This sermon I wrote in twenty minutes from beginning to end. Notice how the Bible verses fit into the story and the vision created a future pace. Notice how the attribution persuasion model was applied in the 'Need' sequence. You'll see many of the Preaching Persuasion Patterns nested throughout this sermon. Notice the hypnotic storytelling and the repurposing of that story into the 'Action' sequence. Notice the parallels of the story with the actions of the subjects; namely: waking up early, making a vow, and feeling blessed. Notice how the artfully vague Milton Model Patterns were applied as well as the Meta Model Patterns. You'll see many times repetition used. You'll see cover embedded commands abundantly utilized throughout this sermon.

This sermon also utilized audience participation to gain compliance. This is extremely important for several reasons: (a) it tells you how impactful your sermon is, (b) it creates a 'yes-set' with the subjects which will persuade them to say yes when the offering plate gets passed around, (c) it further helps you keep their focus on your message and suggestions, (d) it utilizes the persuasion principle of social judgment proof, as well as the influence principles of social proof, commitment and consistency, and liking, and (e) it holds people accountable for follow-through.

Importantly, when you deliver this sermon, like every sermon you give from now on, you must be emotionally and physiologically congruent with the message you are delivering to your subjects. What emotions you elicit to your subjects will be felt by them. When you get to the 'Action' sequence you'll want to be active and convey the motions and emotions of action so you have your audience ready to immediately act—ready to pay their tithes.

What if You Adopt This Approach?

Mainly the benefit gained by adopting this approach to sermon development is you'll consistently be delivering high quality sermons that get you your desired end-results. This method is also easy to construct. You simply use Monroe's Motivated Sequence as the skeleton, and then fill in each sequence with the appropriate persuasion models, vague language patterns, meta-model violations, storytelling techniques, and the preaching persuasion patterns.

Each sermon you deliver will have your audience energized and willing and ready to comply with your requests. When you deliver an alter call, people will be empowered to come and pray for forgiveness. When you deliver a sermon to save the lost, those lost will be persuaded to surrender their lives over to the will of Christ Jesus. When you speak the words of God, your deliver will affect your audience to the extent they will remain with them even after the service is over.

Long term this approach will help you grow your church attendance, offerings, and various church programs. It will create goodwill in your church and keep people motivated to comply with your vision for the church as laid out to you by God.

Chapter Summary

In this Chapter: How To Build a Persuasive Sermon that Moves People & Maybe Mountains, we talked briefly about how we could build a sermon that sells your message in order to be able to insure that we cover all the points that we've mentioned up to this point in the book.

When it comes to persuasive preaching Monroe's Motivational Sequence is the backbone to sermon development. Now this backbone or skeleton is essentially a five sequence delivery system that allows you to persuasively sell whatever the message is you are selling. If you're preaching on 'tithing,' which we covered you're building a sermon around a sequence that is going to have an emotional effect on your audience.

We discussed the five sequences as outlined by Monroe as being: (a) Gaining attention, i.e. where we direct a subject's focus away from everything else your subject is externally or internally focused on (e.g., family problems, money concerns, and so on). We redirect focus onto what we're going to be presenting on. The message we presented in this chapter was 'tithing' and therefore we directed attention by citing an intriguing focus-capturing quote by Voltaire; (b) Next we presented a persuasive question; asking the subjects in our audience to take a side. The need was subtly asserted into the argument when we mentioned tithing in a general sense; (c) Next we brought up satisfaction which was accomplished by telling a beautiful story about Jacob, and how he promised God that he would accept him and when blessed give over a tithe of everything he gained from God to God. This introduced the idea of tithing being associated with the blessings received from God, making the indirect argument that when you tithe you are blessed. (d) Next we had our subjects visualize the future and what it would be like were everyone in the congregation to pay their tithe. This creates massive goodwill with the subject in the presupposition that the monies tithed will in fact go to creating the vision they have in their head. What we do not mention however is that everyone has a different vision when they future pace reality. (e) Next we talked about action and how by taking action and cheerfully giving we are defying the argument Voltaire makes in the quote we cited. So we are repurposing the quote to bring out greater affect in our persuasive argument, while also completing the circle and ending the sermon.

When we talk about a complete sermon it is one that you can actually walk out to the pulpit and begin to deliver the sermon from 'A' to 'Zed', i.e. from beginning to end, until which time it is perfectly presented to assure you the results you expected before delivering it.

Adopting this approach is easy; yet, highly effective in having you achieve what it is you want from your subjects. Cookie-cutter as it may be it works.

After we built the skeleton of our sermon from Monroe's Motivational Sequence we simply applied many of the persuasive elements we've learnt thus far throughout this book. Some of these were the persuasion patterns. Others were the psychological persuasion models and linguistic models from developed from NLP.

Action Steps

The following actions steps are meant to help you bridge the great divide from theory to action. I've heard it said that 80% of self-help books never get read all the way through, and only 20% of people ever complete the action steps found at the end of each chapter. Maybe you've heard of the 80/20 rule:

> *"So the 80/20 Principle states that there in an inbuilt imbalance between causes and results, inputs and outputs, and effort and reward."*

—*Richard Koch*

In other words, 80% of the wealth winds up in the hands of 20% of the population. Twenty percent of products contribute to eighty percent of sales. This statistical discovery has been labeled Pareto's Law, after its founder, Italian economist, Vilfredo Pareto. Pareto in 1906 discovered that 80% of Italy's land was owned by 20% of the population. Significantly, this is found in economics, business, and many other disciplines to ring true; where 20% of some group will benefit from the efforts of the other 80% of the population of that group. These imbalances create leveraged opportunities for those willing to capitalize and do what the 20% does, while avoiding what the 80% doesn't do. I'm sure you can relate this back to one of our persuasion models if you go looking for it.

Suffice to say, I want you to be in the 20% of action takers and gain the true value of what I have to teach you. Certainly the choice is yours, and I'm not there to strike the back of your hands with a rule-stick; however, should you decide to pursue the true value, you'll gain the most, and realize the rewards that 80% percent of the readers won't. Not everyone will be truly great—will you?

I will be repeating this exact same intro to the action steps for each chapter. Do not be alarmed and think I'm doing it on accident to fill up pages. If I wanted to fill up pages, I'd increase the font size and double-space the lines, and add in a bunch of filler; I wouldn't do that to you! Remember back and recall the first words of this chapter:

"Only what we keep hearing do we believe."

—*Bryan Westra*

    I.   Memorize Monroe's Motivational Sequence. Understand what each sequence entails and the various techniques you might adopt for each.

    II.   Create a unique sermon using Monroe's Motivational Sequence as your skeleton. This means using it as an outline for drafting your sermon. Utilize the tool's I've presented you with in this chapter for finding Bible verses. These tools will also give you the ability to cut/paste these relevant verses directly into the various sequences.

    III.   Make your sermon even more persuasive by adding in persuasion patterns, psychological persuasion models and theories, as well as linguist attributes found in the Meta Model and Milton Model. After you are finished, practice your sermon aloud until you have it down and are ready to deliver it. Finally, deliver it to an audience and watch for feedback that tells you how persuasive your sermon is—feedback is very important!

CHAPTER 5

How to Model Persuasive People Magnificently to Break the Persuasion Code

D
rop your guard; you can still be yourself! I'm not suggesting you be a chameleon and mask who you are and become someone else. What I am suggesting is that it is possible to learn and mimic the skillsets and behaviors of other successful people, structurally, and effectively achieve the same outcomes to where they become an unconscious skillset. Replicating a structural process whose code has been cracked lets you duplicate that process and achieve the same consistent results.

Imagine for a moment sitting in a church listening to a preacher present persuasively to a congregation a message. You're observing how much control over the audience this preacher has. It is impressive to you as you sit back objectively and observe the preacher being persuasive from a third-person perspective. In NLP we call this being in the third position where we observe the messenger and the message receiver. We're not being affected like the message receivers are being affected; rather we are objectively sitting on the sidelines taking a survey of the entire scene unfolding. We're not emotionally attached to the message, nor are we influenced by the persuader. No! We're simply sitting back and observing and taking a mental assessment of the audience's reaction to certain specific things the persuader is saying, and eliciting from the audience. We're observing body language. We're observing facial expressions. We're observing other non-verbal forms of communication happening. We're taking note of what is being said, as much as we're taking stock of how it is being delivered by the persuader.

In this chapter we'll travel down this road even further to explore three types of modeling paradigms. We'll tour the analytical or cognitive modeling system, the NLP modeling system, and, lastly, the deep trance identification modeling system.

After you learn how to model greatness in others who are successful you'll be able to add to your repertoire of persuasion skillsets in order to affect change in other people. You'll be able to change minds, beliefs, thoughts, that help people to move more in alignment with the reality you want them to experience. You'll be able to do this because you'll have the unconscious skillsets to exactly do what works in a given situation to persuade someone else to do what you want them to.

Why Model Excellent Persuaders?

Initially this question may seem like a no-brainer. This is because we naturally model people throughout our lives. As a small child your parents and teachers represented models through which you were conditioned to model yourself on or pattern yourself after. You did this act of modeling both consciously through your cognitive mind as well as unconsciously through your other mind. You formed judgments and beliefs around actively watching other people in your reality gain or lose through their actions.

When you noticed someone gaining influence—persuading someone else to take action or do something—you took stock of this and remembered it in case you found opportunity to do the same. Some people, as you got older, seemed naturally more persuasive and influential than others you perceived. At this time in your life you began hearing rhetoric about so-and-so having a gift for gab, being naturally charismatic, a born sales person, a born leader, a person of influence, and so on. You then bought into beliefs, persuaded yourself by what others around you assumed for you to be true, and then told yourself what was true about you. You also took in and believed the advice from others about your own identity. This external definition of who you are by way of the feedback you received from others persuaded you to act in ways that made your beliefs true. This meant for many of you reading this book that you bought into the idea that you had certain limitations and that other people had certain abilities and skillsets which were naturally inherent in them, but which were not in you. This created for you mental limitation. When you became limited by the persuasions of others which were assigned to you by them, already you were being influenced like the audience members you're now observing from an objective third person perspective that I earlier asked you to imagine.

That place of being the audience—you know those folks being persuaded—is known in NLP as the second person perspective. In the world of marketing we might call this our target market. The preacher up there on the platform talking down to the audience is the first person perspective—you know the persuasion artist. These perceptual positions are critical to understand when it comes to modeling excellence.

As a preacher, you might even want to assume anyone in general even, experiences at some point or other in their life any one of each of these three perceptual positions. In life, we are all persuaders in some form or fashion, we're all persuaded in some form or fashion, and we all are third-party innocent bystanders witnessing someone being persuaded by someone else.

To answer the question why; regarding why you might want to model someone who is expertly effective at persuading others, would be to gain the benefit of likewise being able to do the same yourself. It could also be to achieve new persuasion skills you have not yet learned to be able to use them when the opportunity comes around.

What Is Modeling?

There are three types of modeling; namely, analytic modeling or cognitive modeling, NLP modeling, and deep trance identification modeling. Analytic modeling is where there is an expert and an interviewer. The interviewer is asking the expert to elaborate and explain their process for being successfully persuasive. There are limitations to this type of modeling—for example, the exact questions asked by the interviewer can be limiting factors in the explanations given by the expert based on their presumtions. Furthermore, the expert may be expert in their field; however, incapable of articulating consciously what they tend to do without thinking. This means of modeling relies heavily on conscious analysis of the expert. This is the type of learning we gain from conscious understanding of the model.

The NLP Modeling Method might be perceived as a more valuable means by which to model expert persuaders; given it takes into account the unconscious uptake needed to more or less step into the shoes of the model and both consciously and unconsciously model them until results are achieved and within the same time frame of achievement.

The NLP Modeling Method was developed by NLP founders John Grinder and Richard Bandler. Grinder and Bandler modeled three well known psychotherapists achieving similar results, and were able to construct models which were transferable to other psychotherapists; giving them access tools to be able to achieve the same results.

The NLP Modeling Method is a five step process: (a) find and expert to model, (b) arrange to spend time and model the expert (mimicking, observation) more or less at first unconsciously without having to know deliberately what is happening, (c) reach criteria (i.e., after modeling consciously and unconsciously the expert) while continuing to practice unconsciously until at which point you begin to surface some conscious insights, (d) practice recognizing consciously what you are doing unconsciously in order to code the model for transference to others, (e) measure the results of the learners to assess if the model can be construed as a working model.

The last model, The Deep Trance Identity Model, is a method constructed through the works of Dr. Milton H. Erickson. We discussed about him when talking about the Milton Model. Erickson's Deep Trance Identity Model utilizes deep trance in which the hypnotized subject is made to recall everything possible about the expert they wish to model after. During this process the subject is them asked to step into this person, observing the world from their person, thinking what they would be thinking, and acting like they would be acting, and so on. Through this stepping into and identifying process it is said that the other mind of the individual will sidestep conscious analysis and make its own rich understandings. Through this deep trance experience the modeler learns unconsciously what is needed to behave, speak, react, engage, think, and act as if they were the expert themselves.

These three models are all useful and all help individuals to become more persuasively advertently or inadvertently. The NLP and Deep Trance Identification models are perhaps the most useful for purposeful modeling of expert persuaders. Having an intentional discourse with an expert will no less have some benefits in helping you to model them more effectively, nevertheless.

How to Model Expert Persuaders?

When I was twenty, attending university, I was a member of a fraternity. One of the leaders in that fraternity had a certain charisma when it came to influencing the boys and I to study for exams. He was very persuasive and always got his way. People looked up to him, admired him, and we all loved him.

This personality, he had, and way about him, intrigued me so considerably that I began to mentally wonder in those days, "How does he do it? How does he always get us to do what he wants?" My fascination and desire to emulate him grew not out of obsession or a desire to be him; rather, to achieve the same affect he had on me on others. I wanted very much to get my way with the same ease and charisma he was able to achieve.

One night, while on a date with a girl, I modeled my persuasions after him. I discovered myself successful in winning the girl over, though earlier, before the date, I had made up my mind that she was out of my league. By flipping the switch and emulating this fraternity brother, I had gained a huge increase in self-confidence and my ability to communicate without nervousness. It was amazing!

We all naturally, aware of it or not, model other people in various aspects. Simply thinking in my mind, "What would 'X' do?" somehow the answer came and I did exactly that. My results were similar to what I would imagine 'X' would have achieved, had he been on the date with the girl instead of me.

Let's learn exactly how to implement each of the three modeling methods. I'll let you decide which one is your favorite method and how and when to apply each one.

Analytical Modeling Method

Analytical modeling is done through observations; namely, observing recurring patterns that lead to predictive results. Statisticians and mathematicians observe probability measurements to make calculated determinations in much the same way. Modelers of human behavior can observe patterns experts use frequently to gain consistency in their results. When it is determined through repetition that an expert's persuader might say one thing and it have the same effect on his audience, then it possible that when repeated by the modeler that it will have a similar effect.

How you go about learning what these patterns are and to discover how they are useful for an expert persuader is by asking the persuader to elaborate. This is done through an interview-like discussion. Assuming the expert is willing and understands him or herself well enough consciously, this method may produce some rather intellectual results. Then the modeler may go off and practice doing the same, testing the validity of the pattern. If the patter proves effective at producing the same or very similar result of the expert, then it can be shared with others to determine its worthiness as a working model.

This approach, in and of itself, is model framed around critical thinking and analysis. The model is more about probability calculations and less about unconscious learning and adaptation.

NLP Modeling Method

Modeling using NLP's approach is a five step process. This process orientation beginnings by picking a qualified persuasion expert to model. During this phase well-formed outcomes are decided. Once the model has been identified and it has been agreed the modeler may model him or her (i.e., the expert) then the modeling begins by having the modeler watch and mimic everything holistically that the expert does. This form of modeling has the modeler adopting the same physiology, language patterns, mannerisms, values, beliefs, representational systems, so that he or she (i.e., the modeler) can analyze the behavior of the model. During this process preconceived notions are left at bay as internal silence is required. This allows the other mind of the modeler to holistically digest at the unconscious level what needs to be learned in order to likewise be expert. At this stage the modeler is not searching for meaning; rather, observing, listening, mimicking micro-movements over time, and simply modeling what the model does as the model performs in the context he or she is expert in; that is, in this case, persuasion. This stage continues until which time the modeler is unconsciously congruent with the behaviors of the model. Next, the modeler leaves the environment of the model, still modeling at the unconscious level, objectively determining effectiveness, until which time the modeler starts to recognize unconscious patters consciously emerging that let him or her be as effective as the expert modeled. Finally, these patterns are codified and transferred on to other individuals to be tested to fully determine the efficacy of the codified persuasion model.

Many of the persuasion models we have today come by way of this process of modeling. As someone who constantly writes and trains in this niche I am always buying programs and courses on persuasion, sales, influence, and so on. These models of persuasion are engineered into programs that anyone with half-a-brain can understand and apply. Unfortunately, as will be the case most likely with this book, more than 80% of self-help and business books go unread and even more than that unapplied. Don't believe me? Ask yourself when the last time you bought a book, other than this one, and read every word and applied its contents strategically into your career or life. My point precisely!

Let's look at the full process more in depth and how to apply it:

I.   **Choose:** Choosing the right model is rather a subjective undertaking. You want to pick someone who has extraordinary results and someone who is assessable. You might want to choose more than one individual to model to gain deeper insights and better be able to break the persuasion code. In your preaching ministry you'll likely come across many persuasive individuals who you'll share the pulpit with. These could be a great source to pick from when choosing a model to model. One idea might be that you ask to be in their company without going so far as to ask them if you can model them. Asking this of them could make them self-conscious or put-off by the idea and in the process spoil your intentions of successfully modeling them.

II. **Observe:** Observing what someone does without being critical or thinking through their process or forming preconceived notions is

an important step in this process. You have to suspend your disbelief, not form opinions; rather, only mimic and let your other mind
absorb the fine distinction of what the model is actually doing.
These distinctions cannot be gotten consciously; for this reason you
must have an empty mind and simply mimic the model while they
are persuading others. This includes physiologically carrying yourself in the same regard as the model, listening to what they say and
how they say what they say, and model their behavior as exactly as
you can. The best format to use in modeling your chosen model is
through being in their presence and copying what they do. If this is
an impossibility for you the second best solution may be to utilize
prerecorded videos of the model while delivering a persuasive sermon, and so on.

III.   **Practice**: Practicing what the model does when the model is not
around will gain you valuable experience and let you experiment to
determine the necessary mechanics that are attributed to the model
being persuasive. These surface from the recesses of the other mind
over time as you continue practicing and mimicking the model.
Sometimes it may be necessary throughout this practice phase to re-
view stages one and two of this process. Once you compare and contrast start to draw certain conclusions from ongoing modeling of
the model, the persuasion code starts to crack, and you start to have
a improved blueprint that can be useful for consciously and explicitly persuading others at will.

IV.   **Codify**: Codifying the persuasion code means structuring it in such
a way that those who will be benefitting from learning the model
will most aptly be able to learn it. Usually this means a systematic
approach. How you go about this is up to you; however, keep in
mind that there is more than one way to skin a goose. In other
words, be creative and consider your audience and what means will

make what you've discovered as a result of modeling most useful and beneficial.

V. **Measure:** Measuring results means taking stock in how well the model performs by assessing the results other have using it. Poor results may mean you have to reexamine your model. Mediocre results may mean going back and fixing what's not working. In any case the feedback you'll gain will be useful in the perfection of your model.

Deep Trance Identification Model

This last means of modeling has the advantage of being rapid in helping you model nearly anyone you've had exposure to; however, transferring this model on to others is the drawback.

I remember when I was in early elementary school my mother hypnotizing me (she is a hypnotherapist) to step into the shoes of the smartest kid in my class. She had me visualize while in deep trance everything about this student—for example, his mannerisms, his ability to communicate in front of the class and to the teacher, his intense focus during study-time, and his preparedness for class. After the session was over I felt a change happening inside me. I started doing better on my homework assignments. I started focusing more. I began listening better during class. Suffice to say, I became a top student, like the boy I modeled. This was my first experience with deep trance identification modeling.

Since this early experience I have taken to this approach for modeling other highly successful professionals in my niche. The results have been amazing.

So how do you do the same?

The deep trance identification model came about through the works of famed hypnotist Milton H. Erickson. The ability to step into someone else's shoes while under deep hypnosis to the extent that your other mind creates its own rich understandings of the model by sidestepping the conscious mind is an astonishing feat that will help you in so many ways become very much more persuasive in your preaching.

Here's how:

I.   **Deep Trance:** In order to enter into a deep hypnotic trance you can very simply purchase my hypnosis-download by visiting my website: www.indirectknowledge.com. You'll want to purchase the hypnosis-download titled: Deep Trance Identification Modeling. This audio download arrives in your inbox immediately after your purchase. Essentially this audio will guide you step-by-step into a deep hypnotic trance and then walk you through the entire deep trance identification process, which is;

II. **Recollect:** Once you experience a deep hypnotic trance you'll be asked to recall everything you ever experienced about the person you're wishing to model. This will include stepping into their shoes and experiencing the way they see, hear, taste, feel, smell (i.e., sensory acuity), as well as what they think, how they behave, what they believe, and so on.

III. **Total Holistic Immersion:** This third phase has you mentally suspending everything you believe, feel, and presume to be true about reality, and has you sidestepping your conscious reality to become holistically immersed in this person you're modeling. During this phase your other mind will be identifying with them completely; experiencing their world as your own.

IV. **Measure:** Measuring success comes when you are brought out of trance and you intentionally find yourself in a situational context where you will need to be influentially persuasive. In this context you'll determine if your capabilities and results improve or not. Upon improving you'll decipher afterwards if you unconsciously, using your other mind, automatically responded in a way that the individual you modeled would have responded. If you find this method of modeling doesn't work the first time, you may try again, and retest as often as you like.

Some of the known case studies, all of which have been claimed successful, include:

☐ Young men wanting to be more alpha male oriented and less weak and timid around women.

☐ An alcoholic utilizing this process modeled a sober person and himself became in a few months completely free of alcohol.

☐ Athletes have increased their scores and broke records.

☐ Under the supervision of a licensed surgeon a non-surgeon successfully completed a surgery.

☐ A curator of an art museum was able to paint expertly well without ever having painted anything significant before.

There are many examples of where people have modeled the excellence of others using all of these techniques and found themselves improved in areas they wanted to improve in. When it comes to persuasion and influencing others it is worth utilizing these models in order to yourself become more resourceful in your ability to persuade and influence others.

What if You Model Other Persuasive Individuals?

Throughout this book you have learned many models that have been time tested and backed by competent academic research. You've also learned in an active way to apply these models, language pattern templates, blueprints, and theories to be able to immediately take action and be more persuasive in how your preach. If you learn only this you'll be well on your way to being a powerfully persuasive preacher in a relatively short period of time. It's empowering to know this, right?!!

What if you decided to make learning how to be persuasive a lifelong endeavor? I mean, how do you think you'd compare if you knew how to model other expert persuaders and you could create near-perfect models of persuasion for yourself? That would be like teaching you to fish; opposed to just feeding you, would it not?

I think you get the point; however, let me spell it out for you even clearer: I want you to become a modeler. I want you to acquire an internal, unconscious, conscious, means by which you can deconstruct the persuasive elements in every great sermon you hear from this point out in your preaching career.

If you decide to take persuasion to this extreme; that is, utilize the three types of modelling methods I have laid out for you and taught you how to do in this chapter, you'll be able to continually improve your own ability to persuade others. The best part is you'll be able to accomplish growing your church or ministry; bringing more and more people to Christ Jesus, bringing in more dollars so that your church can attract more people, inspire people with your words, and more successfully do the job Christ has called you to do—preach the gospel!

Chapter Summary

This chapter teaches you how to do what I did while doing research for this book. I modeled many of the world's most persuasive preachers and discovered through modeling them what the underlying code to preaching persuasively was all about. The journey I took into their model of the world was beyond spectacular and educational. It gave me inside perspective as to how the most persuasive people in the world make a living persuading others to come to Christ.

This chapter covered in depth the three types of modeling methods I used to crack the code to preaching persuasively so that I could present it to you here. Now, I urge you to do the same, if you choose, and adopt the modeling techniques outlined in this chapter to gain even more insight besides what's in this book.

The first modeling technique we covered was the analytical model. It is a practical and rather more logical approach that only requires you interviewing someone whom you find incredibly persuasive. Modeling analytically is done much the same way a statistician would create a forecast probability; that is, through asking questions and observing patterns that arise. If you talk to enough persuasive preachers and ask them to tell you some of their persuasion techniques, which they use more often than not, you'll discover patterns will emerge. You can then take these patterns and discern which are most effective when it comes to persuading an audience of subjects to take action. This is only one way, however.

The next model we covered originated out of the field of Neuro-Linguistic Programming (NLP) and is a modeling method of five steps; namely: (a) choose, (b) observe, (c) practice, (d) codify, and (e) measure. You first choose a subject worthy of modeling—the most persuasive preacher you might gain access to. Next, you observe without judgment what the model does regarding their physiology, language, tonality, and so on, until which time you begin to achieve the same results as them in the same period of time. You then practice behaving in the same like manner until which time your actions become theirs at the unconscious level. This takes time. After you have gained this type of behavior automatically and are able to persuade people at will without obstacles, you'll start becoming mindful of what it is exactly that allows you to be so persuasive. The next step is to codify the patterns you begin to become mindful of throughout this unconscious-conscious process of discernment. This is when you methodize your conscious understanding of these patterns into a model. You then test the model, and lastly, you pass the model onto others to test to further determine its efficacy. The effectiveness your model has at the end of this process determines if it is reliable enough to personally use on subjects in your church, ministry, or outreach.

The last model we covered is effective on the individual level. You pick a model to imitate in your mind when you are under deep hypnosis. While under hypnosis the hypnotherapist guides you to recall all that you know both consciously and unconsciously about the model. Once you've accessed this, you're then instructed to step-into this model's shoes and become them. During this process you begin to imagine what this person would think; how they might believe; what their map of the world looks like; how do they do what they do when they are being persuasive; and, lastly, you examine their personal history to learn how they got to where they are—you do this all while in a deep trance.

After you've identified with this model on a deep level your other mind starts to integrate the aspects of this person you wish to keep and utilize in your own persuasion situations.

Many people who have adopted this last approach to modeling others have successfully been able to do, for the most part in the same way, what the model seems to do magically and without thinking about. The modeler then finds themselves able to persuade and do in the same fashion, at the unconscious level, what it is they must to gain the same results as the person being modeled.

All three models have their place in the world of advance persuasion pedagogy. In my mind, I see similarities between these three modeling methods and the systematic and heuristic persuasion theories—for example, analytical modeling is very much concerned with the conscious, logical, systematic approach to achieving results; whereas, rather, the NLP and Deep Trance Identification models delve more into the other mind's ability to process learnings and discoveries at the heuristic unconscious processing.

I've now fulfilled my promise to you: I've taken and broken down the persuasion models for you; taught you persuasion patterns and the two NLP blueprints (i.e., Milton Model & Meta Model) as well as expounded on sermon development using Monroe's Motivational Sequences; and then I finally took you full circle back around to how I came up with the information to share with you in this book, that you might, yourself, do the same and learn even more about persuasion and preaching through creating new models and testing their worthwhileness. I hope you've enjoyed this book; rather I should say, I hope you'll use this book and find out for yourself the value thereof.

Action Steps

The following actions steps are meant to help you bridge the great divide from theory to action. I've heard it said that 80% of self-help books never get read all the way through, and only 20% of people ever complete the action steps found at the end of each chapter. Maybe you've heard of the 80/20 rule:

> "So the 80/20 Principle states that there in an inbuilt imbalance between causes and results, inputs and outputs, and effort and reward."

—*Richard Koch*

In other words, 80% of the wealth winds up in the hands of 20% of the pop-ulation. Twenty percent of products contribute to eighty percent of sales. This statistical discovery has been labeled Pareto's Law, after its founder, Italian econ-omist, Vilfredo Pareto. Pareto in 1906 discovered that 80% of Italy's land was owned by 20% of the population. Significantly, this is found in economics, busi-ness, and many other disciplines to ring true; where 20% of some group will ben-efit from the efforts of the other 80% of the population of that group. These imbalances create leveraged opportunities for those willing to capitalize and do what the 20% does, while avoiding what the 80% doesn't do. I'm sure you can relate this back to one of our persuasion models if you go looking for it.

Suffice to say, I want you to be in the 20% of action takers and gain the true value of what I have to teach you. Certainly the choice is yours, and I'm not there to strike the back of your hands with a rule-stick; however, should you decide to pursue the true value, you'll gain the most, and realize the rewards that 80% per-cent of the readers won't. Not everyone will be truly great—will you?

I will be repeating this exact same intro to the action steps for each chapter. Do not be alarmed and think I'm doing it on accident to fill up pages. If I wanted to fill up pages, I'd increase the font size and double-space the lines, and add in a bunch of filler; I wouldn't do that to you! Remember back and recall the first words of this chapter:

"Only what we keep hearing do we believe."

—*Bryan Westra*

I.   Model 'analytically' someone whom you find persuasive. Ask them questions to uncover the secrets behind their success.

II.   Model using the 'NLP' method. Take the five-step journey and model someone you find completely successful. Draw conclusions and code it so others might utilize it and test it to determine its effectiveness.

III. Model using the 'deep trance identification' method. Visualize the person you want to model; captivating consciously, though in trance, everything you may. Then let your other mind process these at the deep unconscious level so they surface once your hypnosis session is over. Notice what happens as a result and determine how much more persuasive you have become.

Bibliography

Cacioppo, P. (1986). The elaboration likelihood model of persuasion. *Advances in Experimental Social Psychology, 19*(1), 123-205.

Campbell, J. (2004). *The hero with a thousand faces* (Commemorative ed.). Princeton, NJ: Princeton University Press.

Chaiken, S., & Maheswaran, D. (1994). Heuristic processing can bias systematic processing: Effects of source credibility, argument ambiguity, and task importance on attitude judgment. *Journal of Personality and Social Psychology, 66*, 460-473.

Chaiken, S., Wood, W., & Eagly, A. H. (1996). *Principles of persuasion.* New York: Guilford Press.

Cialdini, R. (2007). *Influence: The psychology of persuasion.* New York, NY: Collins Business.

Festinger, L. (1957). *A theory of cognitive dissonance.* Evanston, Ill.: Row, Peterson.

G. (2007). *The art of woo: Using strategic persuasion to sell your ideas.* New York: Portfolio.

Ledochowski, I. (2001). *The power of conversational hypnosis.* Washington: Street Hypnosis.

Ledochowski, I. (2003). *The deep trance training manual.* Carmarthen, Wales ;

　　Williston, VT: Crown House Pub.

Murdoch, M. (1999). *The law of recognition.* Denton, Tex.: Wisdom Interna-

　　tional.

Seiter, R. H. G., & John, S. (2010). *Persuasion, social influence, and compliance*

　　gaining (4th ed.) (p. 33). Boston: Allyn & Bacon.

Vogler, C. (2007). *The writer's journey: Mythic structure for writers* (3rd ed.). Stu-

　　dio City, CA: Michael Wiese Productions.

Watts, N. (2006). *Writing a novel: Teach yourself.* Chicago: McGraw-Hill.

Index

ABOUT BRYAN WESTRA

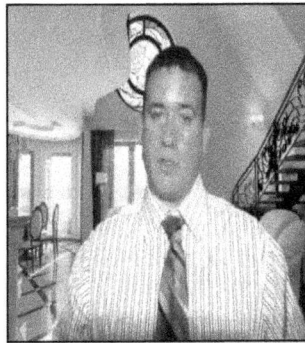

Bryan Westra is founder of Indirect Knowledge Limited
(indirectknowledge.com)

www.ingramcontent.com/pod-product-compliance
Lightning Source LLC
Chambersburg PA
CBHW031808190326
41518CB00006B/241